To The Wild Country

To The Wild Country

John and Janet Foster

VNR Van Nostrand Reinhold Ltd., *Toronto*
New York, Cincinnati, London, Melbourne

ISBN 0 442 29947 8

Library of Congress Catalogue Number 75-5277

Printed and bound in the United States of America

Foreword

John and Janet share with us in these pages remote and hidden places, and the plants, mammals and birds that live there. The television series, *To the Wild Country*, has given them the opportunity to see and film what the vast majority of us will never experience in a lifetime.

What I enjoy most about their work, apart from their creative and technical excellence, is their honesty and integrity. They have not passed themselves off as wilderness dwellers, but as visitors to these remote areas, as we would be. As such, they have captured with unbounded enthusiasm the life and beauty, as well as the ruggedness of Canada's wild places. For example, they invited me to join them on a winter camping sequence in Algonquin Park. They knew, the producers knew, and I knew that no one would know the difference if the scene was filmed fifty feet from the roadside. But, much to my delight, they insisted on trekking deep into a remote spot which they knew and loved, despite the mountain of camera gear and sound equipment that had to go along. I believe this attitude is what marks the difference between a snapshot and a photograph that captures the true spirit of wild places.

John and Janet are also aware of the fragility of wilderness and know the dangers of popularizing these places or of ignoring the ecological sensitivities that must be respected. It is just such a book as this that can increase and strengthen our awareness and create in us a desire and longing for wild places. This is, ultimately, the hope for the preservation of some of the natural world.

Bill Mason
National Film Board of Canada

Preface

Somewhere in a sunrise, a few years ago, we sat in a canoe surrounded by the golden glow of a misty September morning, diligently, almost mindlessly, fishing for trout. We stared into the dark water, somehow unaware that all around us nature was producing great works of art, offering moments of intense beauty for our inspection, and arranging a gallery of exquisite landscapes and miniatures at every bend in the stream. Perhaps the fish were not biting that morning, but all at once we decided we were wasting time. How could one sit there fishing when there was so much to see and photograph? We were ignoring nature at her moment of creation.

To be a nature photographer in Canada is to know the sweet frustrations of living in a land that offers so much. Few other countries have such a marvellous diversity of seasons, geography, wilderness, open space and mood. Canada is a land more than 4,000 miles across, bordered by three oceans, and reaching from the remnant Carolinian forest of Lake Erie to the endlessly beautiful tundra deserts of the high Arctic. The nature photographer looks at the map of Canada with aching desires, seeing a multitude of areas that would take more than a lifetime to explore.

For us, these desires were partially fulfilled with the opportunity to make films about Canada's wilderness, and we found ourselves travelling into some remote and splendid areas, pursuing a project that has brought us three years of hard work and intense pleasure. The purpose of these films was to inspire, entertain, and to give viewers a respect and understanding for Canada's quiet places.

Exploring the far corners of a country that contains some of the last wild places on earth has been an experience that will stay with us for the rest of our lives. We want to share those experiences with everyone who reads this book — to describe some of the images and impressions of an immense land. Indeed, a great many Canadians hunger for knowledge about their country, whether or not they can hope to visit all of its most beautiful areas. For most of us, it is important to learn that, somewhere, unspoiled areas still exist. "Simply knowing it's there", as one writer has said, "is a comfort".

Today we search for wilderness, and almost as soon as we find it, it is wilderness no more. But what is wilderness? You can argue that question for hours. Perhaps we should ask ourselves what level of wilderness experience is necessary to satisfy and replenish our individual needs. For some that level is reached at the summer cottage; others will settle for nothing less than the lonely spaces of the

Arctic, the dark spires of a Yukon forest rising above a glacial river, the scream of a prairie falcon hidden in a deep coulee.

If it was the television series that made this book possible, then we owe a great deal to the people who made the series possible. To Keg Productions Ltd., the producers of the programs, must go the credit for imagination and excellence in the field of nature film making. We are also extremely grateful to the Canadian Broadcasting Corporation for granting us complete artistic freedom in the selection of subject matter and style of presentation. To Canada Trust goes our thanks for sponsoring the series and for giving us professional and enthusiastic support. On location we were constantly advised by biologists, park planners, researchers and private citizens eager to help. Special thanks is due Parks Canada for assigning highly talented planners as our guides and advisors, and for providing many hours of flying time by helicopter into remote sections of northern parks. Speaking as still photographers, we must also pay tribute to the Stills Division of the National Film Board of Canada for its complete dedication to Canadian photographers and for the inspiration it has given to all of us who carry cameras into the Canadian wilderness.

Finally, in the preparation of this book we have had the special assistance of two people. Garry Lovatt, our editor, made suggestions during the writing of the text and spent long hours with us selecting from thousands of colour slides. Donald Chant, Professor of Zoology and Vice President of the University of Toronto, read the final manuscript and gave us the benefit of his expert advice.

In describing six major regions of Canada in this book, we hope to leave you with a sensation of "what it's like to be there" rather than with a detailed, biological description of the land and its wild creatures. We have chosen to describe areas that together represent much of the fabric of Canada — some far beyond the reach of many of us; others within a few hours' drive, yet still breathing of wildness. These are our own impressions and memories of a land we love.

J.F.
J.G.F.

Contents

To The Wild Country

Kluane

On all sides was a chaos of corrugated ice and dark crevasses,
with blue, irridescent pools of melt-water
in every depression.
Mountains rose on three sides;
on the fourth a surprisingly green meadow
stood out in startling contrast.
Twenty miles to the northwest the glacier disappeared
into black storm clouds.

The stubby silver jet began to sigh, losing altitude like a migrant swan searching for a familiar marsh. A lonely forest fire burned in the blue haze below, and in the northwest a distant ridge of sparkling mountains poked into space. Reflections winked and glimmered in the July sun, betraying streams and swamps amid deep stands of black spruce.

From 20,000 feet we stared down in drowsy comfort, trying to imagine great bull moose standing in those spruce bogs, their massive antlers sheathed in velvet. We pictured timber wolves trotting through flaming pink fireweed along the gravel bars of swift, icy rivers, and arctic grayling flashing luminous shades of green and blue beneath every ripple in the clear pools. We remembered bald eagles and osprey patrolling the shallows, and the sudden, icy hailstorm that left a brilliant double

△
Kluane's lowlands include the Kathleen Lakes, clear turquoise waters fringed with spruce trees, bogs and silt beaches. Constantly changing patterns of cloud and shifting micro weather systems are a reminder of the perpetual influence of the mountains.

△
The perfect symbol of Canadian Wilderness — timber wolf tracks on a Yukon sandbar. A pack of eight wolves has passed through here, one of them leaving tracks five inches wide. These sandbars are excellent places to determine who your neighbours are.

rainbow against a black sky—a moment of singular beauty produced as if in apology for the shower. It was good to be back in the Yukon.

The jet found what it was looking for and rumbled on downward. Looking up, we remembered the skies. There is a brilliance to the sun above the 60th parallel that is a startling change from the soft, summer haze of more southerly latitudes. Maybe it is the mountain weather, or perhaps the constantly shifting patterns of light and dark, but a Yukon summer sky reminds you of a child's painting, with clouds standing out sharply against the blue.

In terms of geological time the Yukon is a young land, with powerful and significant wilderness qualities — a land that stretches north from the forests of British Columbia to the Arctic coast of the Beaufort Sea, and includes almost every conceivable type of northern geography. Most of all it is a land of space and solitude, of separation from the urgencies of man's affairs in the south. For those of us who must live in smoking cities it is essential to know that areas like the Yukon Territory still exist. Robert Service spoke for all of us when he wrote:

> *The freshness, the freedom, the farness —*
> *O God! How I'm stuck on it all.*

For anyone who needs the embrace of wilderness, the Yukon has much to offer. On this July day, after a series of hair-raising landings across northern British Columbia, we found ourselves descending towards Whitehorse, carrying 25,000 feet of film, a small mountain of equipment and earnest instructions from our producers about the condition of our budget. During the next four weeks we would attempt to explore and photograph one of the most magnificent areas on earth, Kluane National Park. We carried the usual collection of gear that follows film crews: camera cases, lens cases, tripods, film boxes, tents, freeze-dried foods, sleeping bags, packs and suitcases — a total of twenty-one pieces of luggage, variously plastered with stickers begging the airlines to handle with care and imploring them not to X-ray our film. As it turned out, only one camera case appeared to have been dropped from a height of more than ten feet.

Mindful of the high demand for rental vehicles in northern communities, we moved smartly across the terminal to claim the cars reserved for us. "Cars?", said the clerk. "No one said anything about cars. We have a pick-up truck for you." Five people, twenty-one pieces of luggage, an open truck and a hundred miles of boiling dust and flying stones on the Alaska Highway is a formula that can only produce gritty cameras and damaged equipment. At times like this you persevere. We unleashed our indispensable location manager, Jim McLean, who put on a piercing frown and produced two cars as if out of nowhere. We were on our way.

The Alaska Highway has a life and physical presence of its own. In places it seems to be nothing more than potholes loosely held together with gravel — and much of that gravel seems to stay in constant motion, moving with the velocity of bullets at precisely windshield level. From time to time immense transport trucks thunder past, firing pieces of the road at you and leaving a dust cloud that nothing can penetrate. Add to this a steady parade of large, slow and extremely expensive campers and you begin to get a composite picture of one of North America's most colourful and historic highways. But when the traffic clears, and the dust blows away through the fireweed, you discover that the road north from Whitehorse to Kluane Lake passes through compelling scenery. You also discover that the edge of the road is lined with Arctic ground squirrels who like to stand upright about six inches from where your wheels will pass, and make sudden sprints across the road. Little patches of dusty skin and bone every few hundred feet indicate the odds in this game.

Jim took all of this quite calmly. There are two ways that you can drive on a gravel road. You can move slowly, or you can try to miss most of the pot-holes by flying over them. Jim elected to fly, making our introduction to the Alaska Highway a blur of dust and gravel, and ground squirrels flashing by with shocked looks on their furry faces.

Early in the evening of July 15, we arrived at the base camp of the Arctic Institute of North America, at the south end of Kluane (pronounced kloo-ah-nee) Lake. Its flag, which shows a blue globe favouring the northern hemisphere, flew strongly in the breeze that swept down the Slims River delta from the St. Elias Mountains. This was to be our base for the next three weeks — a jumping off point for trips into Kluane National Park.

We moved into simple plywood shacks, each equipped with two old army cots and a resident family of Arctic ground squirrels beneath the floor. Down at the end of a gravel airstrip, surrounded by flowers, stood the outhouse, equipped with flagpole and a red flag to be hoisted when in use. Rudimentary accommodation perhaps, but with considerably more character and flavour than a worn out motel, of

△
Arctic ground squirrels at Kluane Lake. They are so dense in some areas that one biologist estimated their population in terms of tons per square mile.

which there are plenty along the Alaska Highway.

From this base, the Arctic Institute of North America (a joint Canadian-American organization) is conducting high altitude research in the St. Elias Mountain range. Specifically, this is the Icefield Ranges Research Project, which has the fascinating aim of studying a mountainous region in terms of its total environment. Field parties are moved around and supplied by the Institute's own aircraft, a single engine Helio Courier that has remarkable short-take-off-and-landing capabilites. Studies here have covered such diverse topics as fungi, the breeding territories of song birds, pollination of flowers in alpine meadows, glaciology, medical problems associated with climbing, and the analysis of snow layers on Mount Logan. Students and researchers of many disciplines are flown in and out of remote areas by the Institute to probe Kluane's mountains, glaciers, valleys, rivers, climate and wildlife. Some are accompanied by their families, who must pitch in and help with the daily chores of running the base camp. It is a friendly place, full of enthusiastic, educated young people who love wilderness and believe in what they are doing.

The Kluane landscape is one of wild geographic contrasts and sometimes terrible beauty. Our initial reconnaissance flight confirmed a description from a National Parks planning manual: "The high ice fields are one of the truest wilderness areas remaining in the world today." As we flew through the sudden up-drafts and air pockets of Kluane's valleys, we looked down on blue-green mountain rivers, tundra meadows alive with alpine flowers, and green hillsides dotted with pure white Dall sheep. More often, we found ourselves looking up, for the St. Elias Mountains tower over Kluane, adding their accumulation of snow and ice and rock to the ancient glaciers that grip the valleys like the outstretched fingers of a brooding Arctic god. The icefields here form the most extensive mantle of glacial ice in continental North America, including five of the longest glaciers on earth outside the polar regions. A small aircraft circling Mount Logan is a tiny shape in this immense land. At its base, the massif of Logan is a hundred miles in circumference, and on those days when the mountain isn't busy generating its own storms, you can see the peak (Canada's highest) rising to almost 20,000 feet above sea level. A flight through the icefields and silent peaks which Logan commands can only be described as breath-taking.

▷
Helicopter flights at low altitude along a glacier give one the sensation of following an immense, deserted superhighway through the wilderness. Bob Dunbar loves to fly in such country, and his concern for safety is emphasized by the sign inside his helicopter: "Tail rotors are hazardous to your health".

We quickly came to understand the challenge—and the logistical problems—in filming these 8,500 square miles. Weather permitting, our plan was to shoot seven

CF-DDL

△

A symbolic wedding at 9,800 feet in the St. Elias Mountains. The bride and her fiance were members of a research team that lived here for several weeks. As her wedding dress she wore part of the white parachute that had floated down with supplies for the camp from a Canadian Forces aircraft. After the "ceremony" was shown on television, Parks Canada received eleven requests from couples wanting to be married up in the mountains.

days a week until we had enough strong sequences to make a one-hour film. There is no such thing as a shooting script in areas like this, but Jim McLean had prepared detailed research which identified areas of significant natural beauty, locations that together represented the sum of Kluane's geography and ecological communities. A high priority, as always, was wildlife.

Poring over maps by the light of Coleman lanterns late into the night, assisted by planners from Parks Canada, we began to block out film sequences. For a broad mountain river fed by glacial run-off we chose the Alsek, a powerful, silt-laden river that sweeps across the toe of the Lowell Glacier and rises or falls according to season, weather and temperatures. For alpine meadows and Dall sheep we planned to camp out at 6,000 feet beside the Steele Glacier, hoping that this once famous "galloping glacier" would surge again (it didn't). To capture the power and spectacle of Kluane's mountains we decided to mount a camera with wide angle lens under the wing of the Helio Courier, and fly among the peaks and massive ice fields surrounding Mount Logan. And so it went. Almost every day produced new ideas, changes of plan, sudden instinctive decisions to move one way instead of another, for the film maker's instincts are a vital part of the daily itinerary.

One of our first decisions was to fly with the Institute's remarkable mountain pilot, Phil Upton, on one of his supply missions to "Eclipse", a high ice-field camp at 9,800 feet near Mount Logan. At 7:00 A.M., at the camp on Kluane Lake, Phil switched on the Arctic Institute radio to call Eclipse Camp, seventy miles away in the mountains. "The weather here is roger, roger, roger", came a crackling voice in reply. For more than half an hour after take off we climbed steadily, along the Slims River valley and up the vast, corrugated ice surface of the mighty Kaskawulsh Glacier. On both sides green slopes gave way to shifting gravel, bare rock, deep snow and the ever-present ice. Tongues of glaciers filled almost every valley. Soon we were among the rocky spines of the mountains, with Logan's massif dominating the horizon. As we cleared 10,000 feet, Phil pointed down to some tiny dots of colour behind a cornice at the edge of a thousand-foot drop — the tents of Eclipse Camp, pitched on hard, deep snow in one of the most awesome settings we had ever seen.

Phil checked his wheels to make sure they were retracted above the skis, and began a wide turn between two peaks. Below, a multitude of crevasses appeared as blue chasms in the sparkling snow. Beyond the crevasses he touched down, skis bouncing along an uphill slope towards the cluster of tents. The weather was indeed "roger", and the group who met us were well covered with glacier cream, nose protectors and dark glasses. At 9,800 feet the sun has remarkable strength.

The residents of Eclipse Camp were filled with the sense of wonder that comes from living (even briefly) at this altitude, looking out over the Yukon's most breath-taking mountain ranges. Their mission was largely medical research, under the direction of Major Gary Gray of the Canadian Forces who was studying the causes and effects of altitude sickness. A second purpose of their work was the testing of tents and equipment. Far below their camp, gleaming ice fields and great ridges of sharp rock, etched with deep blue shadows, flowed toward spectacular peaks — Kennedy, Queen Anne, Vancouver and Logan. Some of these mountains were more than forty miles away, but in the clear, cool air they looked like models, perhaps a few hundred yards distant. Only the Helio Courier, passing below us on its return trip like a blackfly alone in space, gave scale to the landscape.

Late that night, as we piled snow around our tent to keep out drafts and marvelled at the silence of the starlit valleys below, the moon began to rise over Mount Kennedy — a moon in partial eclipse. This seemed the perfect salute to Eclipse Camp, for when the camp had been established, several weeks earlier, the sun had been in eclipse.

Next morning we awoke to dense cloud and a forecast of bad weather. Radio chatter went back and forth to Kluane Lake, but there was no hope of a flight out. This was to be the first of several days of heavy overcast, card games and plenty of reading. Spotting a meteorologist's cloud chart in one of the tents, we asked Gary Gray if he had observed many of the cloud forms illustrated. "I've seen them all", he said; "mostly from the inside!" Three days later the weather cleared for a few hours, bringing the welcome sound of Phil Upton's aircraft. But such is the character of mountain weather that even as we left, the clouds were racing in once more, this time for a week.

Once you have flown over Kluane you develop a fascination for the cold beauty and relentless power of the glaciers that grind through the valleys, leaving their eternal mark on the land. Our own fascination almost brought us disaster.

On July 24 we were filming along the Alsek, one of Kluane's broadest and most powerful rivers, a twisting, silt-laden, icy flow of turbulent currents. Deep in the interior of Kluane, the immense Lowell Glacier intercepts the Alsek in a meeting of giants that produces constant erosion along the glacier's wall of blue ice, and a

△
As the ice knuckles over undulations and curves between the mountains, giant crevasses are formed. In summer, below the line of permanent snow, they appear in deadly but startling beauty. Travellers are advised never to cross a glacier alone.

steady supply of icebergs for the river. Few of these icebergs float away; most remain grounded in the silt of the river bed.

The sequence we were filming involved two canoeists who were running the wild rapids of the Alsek. As they reached the toe of the Lowell Glacier, our best camera position was on one of the icebergs. The helicopter was available, and a broad, level iceberg offered a perfect landing site. As a safety precaution the pilot, Bob Dunbar, kept the Jet Ranger idling on its perch while the camera was set up. The two canoeists were to pass along the face of the glacier where they would be dwarfed by the wall of ice and the floes that surround them. We knew the shot would be spectacular and worth the effort.

Suddenly, the canoeists began paddling hard, waving and yelling frantically: "The helicopter, get the helicopter!" A nearby iceberg had suddenly rolled over, and a wall of water was surging towards the iceberg on which the helicopter was parked. Moving with the speed and skill that he had acquired in combat in Viet Nam, Bob Dunbar leaped into his Jet Ranger and brought it to a hovering position, just in time. The iceberg gave a sickening lurch as the water hit. No one went into the river, but it was almost the last straw at the end of a gruelling day. Both paddlers had been in the 34° water a few hours earlier, and both had been rescued promptly by Bob, who had thoughtfully kept a rope sling trailing under his helicopter for just that purpose.

With the determination that is part of his nature, our cameraman, Bob Ryan, calmly finished his shots from the iceberg. It was this kind of persistence that earned him the nickname, "Last Shot Ryan".

Glaciers tend to be alive and dangerous. Only the most foolish explorer attempts to climb across one by himself. As well as the ever-present crevasses, there are delightful little traps called *moulins*, formed by run-off water. These are more or less vertical, narrow, deep, perfectly smooth. If you fall into one without a safety line you have virtually no chance of survival for at the bottom they are generally filled with icy water. With these thoughts in mind we decided to illustrate the climber's technique for escaping from a crevasse. A veteran mountaineer, Monty Alford, drove up to Kluane Lake from Whitehorse to give us a demonstration. On July 30, we flew back up the Kaskawulsh Glacier, hunting for a good crevasse where the ancient, tortured ice had flowed around an unyielding island of rock, or "nunatuk". For safety we stayed below the line of permanent snow where the crevasses are hidden, and chose instead an area where every split and wrinkle in the ice is in plain view.

▷
The splendid and powerful shapes of deeply crevassed ice on the Kaskawulsh Glacier. This immense river of ice is forty-five miles long and up to a mile deep. Future visitors to Kluane National Park will follow a trail to the edge of the Kaskawulsh.

△
An extremely effective camera mount, designed on the spot by cameraman Bob Ryan, and mounted beneath the wing of the Arctic Institute's Helio Courier. A remote switch controlled the camera, and the field of view of the lens was carefully marked out on the windshield in front of Bob's seat so that at all times he could see what the camera was seeing.

We landed among the glowing blue-white sculptures of the silent ridges formed by a bend in the glacier. On all sides was a chaos of corrugated ice and dark crevasses, with blue, irridescent pools of melt-water in every depression. Mountains rose on three sides; on the fourth a surprisingly green meadow stood out in startling contrast. Twenty miles to the northwest the glacier disappeared into black storm clouds.

Monty selected a crevasse deep enough for the demonstration, yet moderately safe to work around. Janet volunteered to do the climbing under Monty's guidance, and as the rest of us planned camera positions, anchored a climbing rope, and concealed microphone cables, she was fitted with her escape harness. Suddenly, the expensive sun shade belonging to the camera bounded away into the depths. Monty promptly lowered himself after it, and began fishing around with an ice axe somewhere below. Nature chose this precise moment to stage an earthquake. The entire glacier shook with a sharp crack, and we were treated to a lightning fast demonstration of how to leave a crevasse. Later we learned that the shock had been felt as far south as Vancouver.

There was an anxious moment as Janet swung out over the crevasse, but she followed instructions carefully and soon learned to manipulate the ropes that were looped around each foot and attached to her harness. The technique is called "prussiking". Every climber working among crevasses must wear these special ropes and be able to climb out alone, while other climbers anchor themselves on their ice axes, taking the strain on the life line that joins all of them together.

The experience was an entirely new one for Janet and she later recorded it in the daily log:

> *They wouldn't let me try a few climbs first, but for freshness and spontaneity filmed the first attempt. All set, cameras go, and I launch myself out and up, and start hauling skywards. With Monty shouting instructions from below I made it to the top, getting soaking wet in the process (and discovering later that my legs were covered with huge mottled black, blue and purple bruises where the ropes had bound).*

The expression of triumph on Janet's face as she climbed over the rim of the crevasse made the whole sequence worthwhile.

Not all of Kluane is ice and rock. The rolling, green slopes that climb away from river valleys have a beauty that is at once both wild and gentle. They are also

◁
Janet learning the art of "prussiking", the mountain climber's technique for escaping from a crevasse. Her right hand is pushing sliding knots up the anchor rope. These knots are part of the ropes that are looped around her legs and feet. She is literally lifting herself up.

remarkably rich in wildlife. This is the land of mountain goats, wandering grizzly bears, whistling marmots and multi-coloured alpine flowers. Moose browse among willows in the valleys and timber wolves range over wide areas. Snow white Dall sheep, the most abundant and visible species, can be seen at long distances, scattered across high meadows like strings of pearls. They are the most obvious beneficiaries of the 1943 legislation that created the Kluane Game Sanctuary and prohibited hunting or trapping in an area of 10,130 square miles. Much of that area is today safely inside the national park (and the rest should be). To see a herd of twenty or thirty Dall rams running free is to understand the wisdom of those who protected this range from the senseless sport of trophy hunting.

Where the waters run clear, fish populations thrive. Arctic grayling, pike, lake trout and even freshwater salmon can be found in the lowland lakes and rivers that drain from Kluane. Some of these rivers flow north, to the Arctic, others south and west to the Pacific, carrying the melt-water from mountain slopes and glaciers, completing the eternal cycle that begins in the sea.

Just as the mountains dominate the landscape, so do they control the climate in Kluane. Standing as a barrier between the interior and the Pacific, the mountain ranges block the moist and moderating influence of the ocean, forcing weather systems to discharge their moisture along the western ridge of the barrier, and leaving the Kluane area, on the other side, with a relatively dry climate. On the Alaska side of the mountains precipitation may reach 125 inches a year, but at Kluane Lake, just over a hundred miles to the east, about fifteen inches is the average. It is this tremendous discharge of moisture in the St. Elias Mountains that has maintained the great snow and ice accumulations that date back to the earliest years of the last ice age.

Hikers who have been consistently rained upon in Kluane may wonder at that figure of fifteen inches. We were convinced that the year's entire fifteen inches fell on us in three weeks. Perhaps, like the cartoon character, we moved around with a perpetual thunder storm above us. More likely, we were ignoring the character of mountain weather, which constantly produces micro-systems and extremely localized showers. But surely all of these phenomena simply add to the many fascinating dimensions of a journey through the Kluane wilderness. The sky is rarely still. At one glance you may see sunlight, rainbows, snow squalls and rainstorms. You may suddenly be soaked and just as quickly dried. And if you are a

▷
High ice fields of the St. Elias mountain range, near the Alaska border. These immense and ancient areas of snow and ice accumulation form a high barrier between the Pacific Ocean and the continental interior. Five major glaciers have their origin here, and thirteen peaks rise higher than 15,000 feet.

photographer you will begin counting every remaining roll of film, for the appeal of these landscapes is irresistible, with their ever-shifting cloud formations moving, changing, painting the land with patterns of light and dark. Above and beyond all of this is the constant presence of the St. Elias Mountains, reaching to the sky in a white sea of silence.

It will be some years before Kluane is finally "planned" and developed as a national park. Hopefully, this superb landscape will not be scarred by too many access roads. Kluane is a place for hiking, climbing and solitude, a relatively primitive area that should be permitted to remain primitive as a lasting example of Yukon geography. However, the park's initial boundaries are a compromise of those old conflicting interests in the north — beauty and the buck. The park is magnificient, but huge areas of adjacent land were excluded when a powerful mining lobby objected (even though commercial mining ventures here have varied from limited success to financial disaster). From the standpoint of future use, and the possible impact of large numbers of visitors, Kluane will face problems unless boundaries are enlarged. Over half the park is ice and rock — spectacular, but inaccessible for most people — and a large part of the remainder is very steep. Valleys, the usual target of casual hikers, are in shorter supply. The most immediately accessible areas will undoubtedly get the most use. And several vital wildlife areas have been excluded, notably the mountain caribou range, some high quality Dall sheep range, and a wolf denning area. Kluane Lake itself is outside the park, and thus not protected by the stringent laws governing land use in national parks. The expansion of Kluane's boundaries to include these areas is a high priority among those who understand the urgency of wise land-use planning in the north.

We left Kluane reluctantly, vowing to return, to spend time quietly hiking in some of the splendid areas we had glimpsed during a hectic three weeks of filming. Perhaps the essential appeal of the park is the feeling that you could spend half a lifetime exploring there, returning again and again, never growing tired of a landscape that changes constantly. There are few places in Canada that offer more to the wilderness traveller.

2▽
3▷

4▽
5▷

6▷

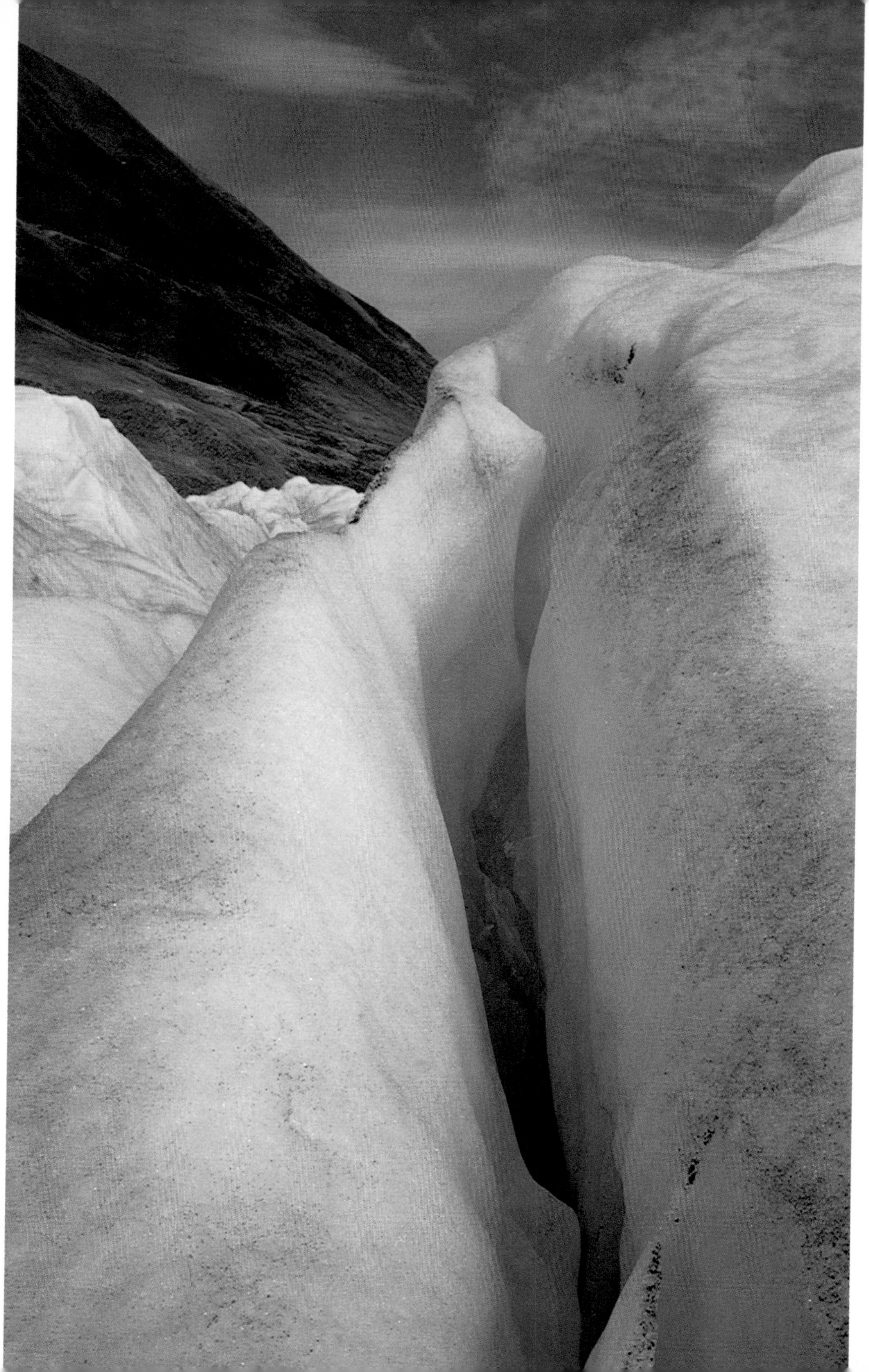

7▽
8▷

Wild Pacific Shore

In front of us, on a high rock bluff,
was a rare peregrine falcon
silently watching.
To the right, circling in the sky on wind currents
that swept up the island's high cliffs from the sea,
were five bald eagles. And behind us were colonies of bellowing sea lions. . . .
We looked at each other and knew
why we had come to Triangle Island!

The secluded beach on Wya Point is deserted. It is early May and too soon in the year for summer tourists. New life surges and pulses in every hidden nook and cranny along the rocky shoreline. Intertidal pools glow with brightly coloured starfish and sea anemones. A young mink frolics across the warm sand and wriggles his way under volcanic rock in search of crustacea and mussels. Above, a bald eagle watches from her nest, studying the mink's every movement with interest. Groups of sandpipers sweep low over the beach, and black oystercatchers flutter urgently along the rocks, their whistling cries carrying clearly above the roar of the surf.

It is springtime — the very best time of year to be on the west coast of Vancouver Island.

△
Long fingers of dark cloud move in from the Pacific at the start of a three day storm of high winds and driving rain over Triangle Island. Winds here frequently sweep in at more than a hundred miles an hour.

△
In the deep shade of ancient firs and cedars there is intense competition for light and space. A tiny fern catches a few moments of sunlight among the immense trees of a west coast rain forest.

Long before the spring tides began to sweep in from the Pacific, we had begun our preparation, spreading out maps and trying to digest thirty-nine pages of research prepared for us by our ever-enthusiastic location manager, Jim McLean. Every page spoke of the drama of Canada's western shore, of wildlife nourished and embraced by the temperate climate of that unique region between the mountains and the edge of the sea. Braving the misery of seasickness, Jim had travelled by small boat to offshore islands where one can glimpse the volcanic origins of Vancouver Island among the black spines of rock that seem to be emerging only now from the sea. And somewhere to the north, he told us, was an uninhabited and virtually inaccessible island swept by gales and defended by reefs on every side, but known to be the most exciting colony of ocean birds and mammals off the west coast. "It's called Triangle Island", he said, "but I doubt if you'll be able to get there." While noting the challenge, we turned our attention back to the more accessible but still spectacular region that forms the heart of Pacific Rim National Park.

Pacific Rim is a long coastal park including some ninety-eight offshore islands and embracing superb sandy beaches, coves and rocky inlets between Ucluelet and Tofino on the west coast of Vancouver Island. The park also includes some of the last original rain forests in British Columbia.

Just outside Ucluelet we shouldered our packs and followed the mile-long trail to Wreck Bay and Wya Point. We wound our way through the thick undergrowth of a typical west coast rain forest, and over boggy ground covered with mosses, skunk cabbage and crumbling fallen limbs. Long tendrils of moss hung down languidly from knarled, ancient trees, some of them 800 years old. It was a silent world of light and dark contrasts, of tiny seedlings, young ferns, wisps of moss and delicate cobwebs.

Rain forests are a unique result of the sea's influence on the land. Winds sweep across the great expanse of ocean and rise up against the mountain ranges. There they are chilled, releasing their moisture in heavy rains that average 122 inches a year in the Long Beach area. These abundant rains are the lifeblood of the island's thick, heavy vegetation. Huge trees — cedar, western hemlock, Sitka spruce, Douglas fir—some of them towering 200 feet or more, grow in dense stands. There is tremendous competition for light and space in the rainforest; everything grows on or out of everything else. Old trees topple and decay, providing a nursery for hundreds of tiny seedlings in their rotting bark. Generations later the nurselogs are gone, but the trees they have nourished stand in straight rows marking the place where the nurselogs once lay.

The Pacific dominates and characterizes this land, providing a richness of marine life along the coast to challenge any photographer. Intertidal pools cradle myriads of delicate sea anemones, starfish of every colour, spiny sea urchins, limpets, clams, hermit crabs and long sea cucumbers—a perpetual food source for countless bird and mammal species that find life between the tides.

Bald eagles face extinction in most regions of North America but on the Pacific coast they thrive on a diet of fish and crustacea in one of the last North American coastal environments that is still relatively wild. We had never seen so many bald eagles. There was an inhabited nest on almost every point of land, and they patrolled the beaches constantly, eyeing the tides for an easy meal or strutting along the sand examining dead creatures presented by the sea. On one occasion we counted sixteen bald eagles circling in the wind currents above us, swooping on each other in play, rolling over in the air and diving low among the trees in an effortless display that seemed to symbolize the freedom of an easy life.

Off the shores of Long Beach, within easy sight of land, California grey whales migrate each year up the coast to Alaska from their breeding grounds off Baja California. Surprisingly, and to the delight of local biologists, a few stay at Long Beach throughout the summer. Most evenings you can see them, clearly outlined and back-lit by the setting sun, rolling and blowing in Wickaninnish Bay. And scan the Sea Lion Rocks, just off Long Beach, with a pair of binoculars; you'll see huge sea lions plunging through the surf or lolling on the rocks.

We explored and filmed among the offshore islands and coastal solitudes of Pacific Rim National Park for two weeks, leaving only when a sudden weekend flood of campers invaded the region, reminding us that the newly paved road from Port Alberni has become an irresistibly easy route to stretches of sand that were once remote. Long Beach became an incredible twelve-mile parking lot, a chrome jungle of camper trailers, vans, open convertibles, pick-up trucks and noisy wandering motorcycles — the whole area illuminated by strings of campfires. Yet, less than three miles away, lonely beaches protected by a barrier of dense rainforest remained undisturbed, as few people ventured far from their cars. The problems of over use are concentrated in one area along the beach that has quickly become all too famous. We began to think wistfully of uninhabited and inaccessible Triangle Island.

△
Shooting incoming surf on a west coast beach. The long lenses will lend drama to the scene by making the waves seem both taller and closer together. From the left: John Foster, assistant cameraman Cam McDonald, cameraman Bob Ennis, and John Boren, a hitchiker who joined the crew as sound man, pack hauler and camp cook.

△
Patterns between the tides on a Vancouver Island beach — a place to run barefoot, recalling childhood memories of sun, sand and salt water.

▷
Triangle Island rises from the Pacific at the western edge of the Cape Scott Islands. It is steep and treeless, towering above its own narrow beaches and rimmed with jagged rock shoals — but throbbing with a marvellous variety of wildlife.

"Triangle Island? It's a miserable pile of rock": an earthy opinion from a west coast fisherman. For us, though, every new story about Triangle sharpened our instincts and increased our determination to get there. We heard of bald eagles nesting on pinnacles of bare rock; of sea lions and harbour seals; of tufted puffin colonies, murres, auklets, and cormorants nesting on cliffs and sheer rock faces; and of rare peregrine falcons. But logistical problems and other seemingly insurmountable obstacles lay between us and Triangle, almost convincing us the island was, indeed, impossible to reach.

Triangle lies sixty-five miles off the northwest coast of Vancouver Island, a huge wedge of rock thrusting up out of the Pacific at the end of a long chain of islands and reefs known as the Cape Scott group. It is a wild, lonely place. Legends are told about the sudden storms lasting days, or even weeks; of the lighthouse that blew over in 1917, its instruments recording wind speeds of 145 mph before it fell. (Winds frequently reach that velocity in the Cape Scott region, but the story of the lighthouse blowing over turned out to be only a legend—it was dismantled in 1917.) Many people doubted we would be able to get to the island, let alone back again. But nothing succeeded in dampening our enthusiasm to go, not even the possibility of being stranded there.

We knew a guide would be needed and were soon put in touch with Frank Velsen, a government fisheries biologist stationed at Nanaimo. Frank had been to Triangle four times, exploring and mapping the island thoroughly. Most important, he knew the location of nearly all the bird colonies. During his previous trips to Triangle Frank had developed a very special interest in the island, and when we asked him to go with us there was no hesitation in his reply.

Frank added his warnings to all the others we had heard. It was difficult, if not impossible, to land a float plane among the reefs of Triangle and pilots were understandably reluctant to test the swelling tides and dangerous winds. He conceded that a fishing boat could ferry us across from Winter Harbour, a tiny fishing port on the north coast, but it would be a sixty-five mile trip over one of the most infamous stretches of the Pacific. If the wind was up—as it usually is—there was no guarantee that we would get ashore safely. In spite of all these warnings Frank shared our eagerness to go.

An entire day spent by John on the telephone to various helicopter and small aircraft companies, to the Canadian Forces Base at Esquimault and the Department

of Transport at Prince Rupert, was finally rewarded with an offer from the Canadian Coast Guard. They were planning to work the area of Triangle around June 5 with a huge Sikorsky helicopter and would lift us *off* the island if we could find our own way there. With a return trip virtually guaranteed, getting out to Triangle no longer seemed a problem — or so we thought.

More phone calls were made, this time to the fishing co-operative at Winter Harbour. Otto Botel, a summer salmon fisherman there, had a sturdy little vessel and was not in the least intimidated by the prospect of crossing to Triangle. It was now Wednesday, May 28, and we made an arrangement to rendezvous with Otto in Winter Harbour on May 30.

Gentle morning breezes were blowing when we flew north out of Tofino by float plane on the Friday, but two hours later, when we touched down in Winter Harbour, the gentle breezes had turned to gale force winds. We soon learned that our chances of going to sea that afternoon were slim. Otto confirmed the reports. It was calm in harbour but outside, he told us, the sea was "standing on end".

Winter Harbour is really a summer harbour, a sheltered cove tucked inland about eight miles from the open sea and used by visiting fisherman during the height of the salmon season. The permanent community is small. There are no hotels or motels, not even a restaurant. Fisherman live on their boats, selling their catch and buying supplies at co-operatives situated right on the wharf. The tiny community, surrounded by rolling hills and seemingly far removed from Pacific storms, provided an idyllic setting. We were stranded there for at least one night but a young couple took pity and offered us their warm hospitality, and a resting place on their living room floor.

At four o'clock the next morning most of the fishing boats were getting ready for departure. Lights winked through the darkness and shadowy forms scuttled to and fro preparing lines and nets for the day's fishing. We filed on board Otto's boat optimistically but twenty minutes out of port, en route down the channel to open sea, the waves grew bigger until our hapless boat bounced and bobbed about in a most disconcerting manner. Our cameraman, Bob Ennis, was turning white but Otto, his eyes twinkling, delightedly told us landblubbers that we were not even past the headland yet. One look at the angry storm clouds gathering ahead convinced us to abandon the mission and return to harbour.

It was a dismal returning. Six o'clock in the morning is a cold, damp time of day in Winter Harbour. Getting to Triangle was going to be a lot harder than we had

◁
Northern sea lions loafing along the rocky shore of Triangle Island. They growl and roar constantly and appear clumsy on land. Once in the water, they swim easily and gracefully. Many are illegally shot by fishermen who consider them unfair competition.

△
H.M.C.S. MacKenzie *anchored at Winter Harbour, a remote fishing and logging community on the north end of Vancouver Island. Fifty miles of stormy ocean were blocking our way to Triangle Island, and we tried unsuccessfully to persuade the captain of the* MacKenzie *to take us there.*

thought. Otto told us the sea could take another three days to settle down. Prospects looked gloomy indeed.

Over breakfast John casually glanced out the co-op window and there, to his astonishment, was a destroyer, H.M.C.S. *MacKenzie*, steaming majestically into harbour with ceremonial flags waving and bearing (as we soon learned) the Lieutenant-Governor of British Columbia on a courtesy call to Winter Harbour. It took only a second to realize that such a powerful ship could easily get us to Triangle!

We dashed down the wharf to where the Lieutenant-Governor's party was already coming ashore. There was little time to talk, but one of the official aides told us the destroyer had moored the previous night in the Cape Scott region, dropping anchor not far from Triangle. He advised us to have a word with the Captain on board ship. Nothing ventured, nothing gained. We hailed the ship's launch and were soon heading out to the destroyer anchored in the bay.

The ship's Captain, Commander Sweeney, was friendly but regretful: if only they had known the previous night, he said, nothing would have given them greater pleasure than to have taken us to Triangle. But now their schedule was tight and, unless the Lieutenant-Governor could be persuaded to change his plans, they would have to move on. We decided on an appeal to the Lieutenant-Governor.

One hour later, still hopeful and dressed in slightly cleaner shirts and jeans, we mingled with smartly uniformed officers and beautifully dressed ladies at an official reception. We made a thorough nuisance of ourselves, pestering every officer in sight. We talked to the Lieutenant-Governor's most senior aide, but it soon became obvious the *Mackenzie* could not take us to Triangle. What a marvellous film sequence it would have made — out to Triangle by destroyer! A friend later said: "You two won't stop at anything, will you!" We didn't and wouldn't, we were that determined to get to Triangle Island.

Our persistence finally brought results. At the reception we were given the name of a helicopter pilot who was working nearby. A quick phone call brought immediate confirmation that he and his "chopper" were available at a cost still within our budget. Arrangements were made immediately. Our expedition to Triangle was at last becoming a reality.

At eight o'clock the following morning, the helicopter was carrying us out over the Cape Scott chain of islands and one of the worst stretches of sea for wind and tides on the whole of the west coast of British Columbia. It was a slow flight, for our small craft was battling fierce head winds and weighted down by two huge plastic containers of fresh water. (Frank had reminded us there was no fresh water supply in the island.)

Triangle is, indeed, a triangular hunk of rock, rising some 500 feet out of the sea. Flying over it we were struck by the total absence of trees. Grassy green-banked walls rose from the beach to a flattened top covered by densely growing salmonberry bushes. We could see where the lighthouse had stood until 1917. Some said the light frequently could not be seen because it was above the fog! Below the plateau were rocky beaches littered with logs and timbers washed ashore over many years — some of the famous "wooden beaches" of British Columbia. As we descended, hundreds of seabirds wheeled and circled, sea lions basked on the outer rocky islands, and we could see on at least one bare pinnacle what looked like an inhabited eagle's nest.

Triangle was all that we had imagined. In fact, it was more, far wilder than we had dared to hope. Harbour seals were our most frequent visitors, bobbing up and down in the waves and staring at us with curiosity, their large eyes and shaggy whiskers giving them a serious, yet comical, expression. We shared one end of the beach with three pairs of black oystercatchers, beautiful black birds with pink feet, bright red beaks and red-rimmed eyes. Approach within fifty feet, and they sound a general alarm for the whole island. A pair of bald eagles nested on a pinnacle of rock some 300 yards down the beach. Climbing an adjacent peak, about 200 feet from the nest, we could see two young eaglets. Both parents flew in circles over our heads, giving short, anxious calls, but they eventually returned to care for the young.

A grassy spot well back from the beach logs made an ideal tent site. On our first night we lay in the sleeping bags totally mystified by whirring, plopping and shuffling sounds all around us. A flashlight shone outside soon revealed Cassin's auklets returning to their colonies after spending the daylight hours at sea. We had pitched the tent right at the edge of grasses concealing their burrows. Cassin's auklets are small, dark grey in colour, and have a distinctly fishy smell. They also have a habit of disgorging partially digested fish when disturbed or frightened. During the night a few of the birds mistakenly glanced off the soft sides of our tent and next morning we discovered little mounds of fresh, pink, smelly, second-hand fish on the ground. It was a marvellous introduction to the island, but we moved the tent right after breakfast!

△
Gulls that nest among other species of sea birds tend to develop strong predatory habits. These glaucous winged gulls were sharing cliff ledges with Triangle Island cormorants and were apparently unpopular.

△
Bald eagles go through life being harassed by smaller birds. These glaucous winged gulls on Triangle Island objected strongly when an eagle perched too near their nesting territory, swooping so close to his gleaming white head that he literally flinched each time.

Our first encounter with the sea lions came later that morning. Walking to the extreme end of the beach, we rounded a rocky point of land and climbed down into a series of coves and small bays. Just offshore, a rocky island was almost completely covered with sea lions. The bulls, weighing up to half a ton, each one surrounded by its harem, rocked back and forth on their front flippers, thundering out their dominance. The grunting, growling, bellowing sound, which we later recorded with a parabolic microphone, was quite incredible.

We filmed quietly and then crawled back along the ledges and up among the rocks to the beach. John suddenly grasped my arm. In front of us, on a high rocky bluff, was a peregrine falcon silently watching. To the right, circling in the sky on wind currents that swept up the island's high cliffs from the sea, were five bald eagles. And behind us were colonies of bellowing sea lions. What a magnificent place! We looked at each other and knew why we had come to Triangle Island.

For the next few days we filmed as much as we could of the island's unique wildlife. The hills behind our campsite were full of tufted puffin colonies. For much of the day most of the puffins stayed underground, brooding their eggs, but late in the evening, just as the sun went down, they would suddenly burst forth from the burrows. In what seemed to us joyous flights of exultation they swooped low over the sea or climbed high on the winds, plummeting back to earth again like little bullets. It was a happy sundown ritual.

Not all evenings were so pleasurable. For the fifth day of our stay an ominous entry appears in the daily log:

> Monday, June 6, 8:00 A.M. *Rained hard and blew all night. A dark, grey day with heavy mist rolling in from the sea. Get up reluctantly and coax a fire into life at main camp. Bacon and eggs with hot toast and tea help lift our dampened spirits.*

It remained dark all that morning and by eleven o'clock the heavy, driving mists turned into equally heavy, driving rain. Mother eagle stood stoically on her nest atop the craggy peak, with wings slightly spread to shield the two young ones lying at her feet. She held that position for the next twenty-four hours, always keeping her back to the wind—a living weathervane lost in the mists above us.

All the other creatures on the island seemed to enjoy the bad weather. Harbour seals dived among the waves, pausing occasionally to peer at us; puffins flew in and out from their cliffside burrows behind our campsite, and oystercatchers whistled continually. Throughout the day the weather continued to deteriorate:

Monday, June 6, 6:00 P.M. *Looks just like it did at 6:00 A.M.—howling winds and rain. Build another huge fire; fortify our lagging spirits with more hot tea and cold sandwiches. No improvement to weather or spirits.*

Wind continues to blow, mist/rain falls, and sea storms. Sighted sea lions and lone harbour seal close to shore—porpoising and rolling in the waves. Seem to be having the time of their lives (wish I was a sea lion).

That night the wind howled, the sea moaned and Cassin's auklets filled the darkness with their strange pulsing sounds. At four in the morning the camp looked very bleak and we began to remember the stories of "sudden storms" that could last for days. Later, over breakfast, each of us endeavored to remain cheerful. Eventually we decided to make the most of a rotten situation by filming the misery of our storm-swept campsite. Bob Ennis tied a plastic bag around his camera in an attempt to keep it dry and shot us from the sheltered entrance of Frank's tent. There we were, bundled up in full rain gear, eyes streaming from campfire smoke, sipping mugs of coffee and listening to the occasional "squish", "squish", from Frank's sodden running shoes. We were also listening for another sound, for this was the day the Coast Guard had promised to lift us off.

Filming was almost finished when, to our great relief, the huge Sikorsky helicopter arrived, rotors spinning a great hoop of water in the sky. Landing was obviously going to be a problem. We marked a likely spot on the beach but the pilot evidently did not like either the terrain or the dangerous down-drafts from the rocky walls behind. After some hesitation, he chose a landing spot on a sheltered beach behind the cliffs and far from our campsite. Frank climbed over, returning soon with hurried instructions to pack all our gear.

We scrambled—pouring out the fresh water, dousing the fire and throwing everything together hastily in anticipation of a speedy departure. Too hastily. While we were packing the helicopter rose and disappeared into the storm and mist across the sea. We assumed the pilot was going for fuel and would return. We continued throwing our gear together, piling it up in a sodden mound on the beach and then huddling under tarpaulins to wait for the Sikorsky to reappear.

Hours passed. Rain seeped into our clothing, our packs and our spirits. Every rumble of the surf became the sound of a returning helicopter. But by six o'clock Triangle Island was enveloped once more in the fog, and we realised with sinking hearts there could be no helicopter that day. We would have to set up camp again.

△
When biologist Frank Velsen began exploring a rocky ledge above a Triangle Island beach he was met by an annoyed bald eagle that was nesting on an adjacent pinnacle of rock. Within hours the eagle had grown accustomed to our presence on the beach below.

Our gear had been packed so badly that everything was now either wet or damp — sleeping bags, clothing, even the insides of the tents. At nine o'clock that night we crawled into our bags, cold and worried by the knowledge we had only a limited supply of food. We wondered what had happened to the helicopter. Had it crashed into the sea?

A night of torrential rains and gusting winds was followed by yet another typical Triangle morning — dark, foggy and drizzly. John retrieved a pack from the beach and found some cheese and hard chocolate concealed in the bottom. Such a howl of joy went up from all of us that John declared he felt like the liberating forces bringing relief to starving refugees.

At four o'clock in the afternoon the winds finally changed. The storm cleared away, revealing for the first time in three days a blue sky and sparkling sea. We grabbed our cameras and made for the eagles' peak.

Once again we climbed the adjacent cliff about 200 feet from the nest. From this vantage point we had a good view and were able to film the family without crowding them. The young were still lying in the bottom of the soggy nest. Occasionally they stood up and we could see both were very wet. They must have had a miserable three days. We stayed just long enough to get the important footage of the eagle family. Nor did we have long. As we finished, the heavy storm clouds rolled over once more and the rains pelted down again. But now it no longer mattered. The bad weather that had delayed our departure had proved to be a blessing in disguise, for we had captured precious moments of the eagle family on film.

Next day we found ourselves once more staring into a Pacific storm and listening hopefully for the sound of throbbing engines above the gale. Finally, late in the day, came the sound we were waiting for. Within an hour we were up and away, heading back through the storm towards Vancouver Island. We looked back once into the mist, but Triangle Island was gone.

▷
The "broken islands" of Barkley Sound. Some ninety-eight of these islands are included in Pacific Rim National Park. Most are quite wild, and offer shelter from the Pacific, with a splendid view of Vancouver Island's west coast. They are a major addition to Canada's system of national parks.

Of all the regions we have filmed in Canada, Triangle and the west coast stand out most vividly in our memories. Part of the reason lies in the character of a coastal environment that shelters and nourishes such an abundance of life. All the rain and wind and dark days of Triangle did not obscure the island's lonely beauty, nor

detract from the excitement and the experience of being there. For us, Triangle, with its nesting bald eagles, peregrine falcons and noisy colonies of seabirds and sea lions, remains a symbol both of the richness of life on the west coast and of the wildness that still remains.

1∇

2▷

3▽
4▷

5◁

6▽

7▷

8▽
9▷

Short Grass Country

If you linger at the edge of the Red Deer River,
you will hear packs of coyotes howl to each other
in evening communion,
their calls and answers echoing
across the badlands,
enticing the listener to join in.

There is a common belief among those who don't live there that the western prairies are vast, flat, vacant plains rolling monotonously away under an endless sky and baking summer sun—an area to be endured, if not avoided. Travellers from the east leave the green forested hills and silent lakes of Ontario and Manitoba reluctantly. They speed along the Trans Canada ribbon of highway scarcely bothering to look left or right, their minds firmly fixed on the Rocky Mountains beckoning in the distance. Others, loath to waste precious holiday hours on the "empty" plains, fly directly to Calgary and with just a hasty backward glance, head immediately into the foothills. The dull western prairies are best forgotten.

This common belief is only a myth. True, the prairies do seem to roll endlessly under a sky that stretches in a great blue dome from horizon to horizon. And in the summer, the sun does beat down relentlessly on an arid land. But the prairies are far

△
Late in the afternoon mule deer emerge from the shelter of the aspen forests and deep gullies of Alberta's foothills to steal a feed of oats from a tolerant farmer. They are distinctly nervous when in the open and if startled will quickly jump away with a rapid, bouncing gait. The grain is swathed and drying, awaiting the combine.

△
In late September waterfowl gather across the prairies and move slowly south, resting and feeding among the prairie potholes, and mingling with cattle on the open range. Giant Canada geese are being re-introduced in some areas and spend the entire summer here.

from vacant. Reduce your speed, turn off the Trans Canada Highway, as we did, and take the dusty sideroads that wind through fields, past gentle hills and bushy coulees, into the southeast corner of Alberta, and you will soon find how full of life these prairies really are. In June almost every fencepost comes equipped with a singing meadowlark, ducks and shore birds wade and nest in every pond and pothole, and ground squirrels scamper busily about in the roadside grasses.

This is a unique land—short grass country—part of the great central plain of North America that stretches from the Gulf of Mexico up into Canada's prairie provinces. Hundreds of species of native grasses support and nourish an abundance of bird and mammal life. Ask any rancher and he will tell you that Nature knew best, that these original grasses co-exist in a mutually beneficial community, holding the dry soil together, supporting tiny wild creatures and grazing animals through sometimes appalling conditions of wind and drought. Run your fingers through these tough little grasses and you might question their reputation. Yet one grass supports another: tall ones give protection against the sun's burning rays; shorter species spread over the surface in a protective mantle, hugging the soil and holding precious moisture. These are complex communities that the ranchers respect; even today the plough is used sparingly and sometimes not at all.

"All flesh is grass", goes the old saying. Indeed, the chain of life begins here, flowing from the grasses to the small rodents who draw nourishment from them—little creatures like pocket gophers, deer mice, ground squirrels—who are in turn eaten by such predators as golden eagles, foxes and coyotes. In this way, life and energy flow from the prairie to the larger mammals and birds of prey.

It has been said the buffalo was the first good judge of grass. Between forty and sixty million of these shaggy monarchs once roamed the plains of central North America, grazing the land and keeping the grass short — hence the term "short grass" country. Today, herds of cattle have replaced the buffalo, converting these same prairie grasses into expensive beef steaks for urban markets.

If you want to feel the real thrust of history, go to the badlands of Alberta's Dinosaur Provincial Park, north of Medicine Hat, where the land shows its bare bone. It is hard to believe, standing in the intense summer heat on a strangely eroded landscape, that this was once a great salt water swamp, the edge of an ancient, continental sea. Huge reptiles and dragon-like creatures hunted across the marshes and lumbered ponderously over the land, and here the dinosaur made his last stand.

Dinosaurs disappeared forever from the face of the earth sixty-three million years ago. Since then glaciers have surged down from the north and scoured the land; wind, water and frost have worked their way into beds of soft shale, sandstone and clay, gouging the terrain and carving a silent, nightmarish world of tall "hoodoo" clay columns and weird sandstone cliff formations. These primeval forces of erosion have bared the land's age old secrets. Mineralized dinosaur bones and vertebrae lie scattered among chunks of petrified wood and lichen-covered stones. When we climbed the tall columns and sandstone pillars we were amazed to discover fish teeth, a reminder of marine life that swam on the plain that was once a swamp, 135 million years ago.

The hills, gullies and scorched white cliffs of the badlands blaze and bake in the noonday sun. At first glance, it seems as though all life disappeared with the dinosaur for the park appears strangely silent and empty. But listen and watch awhile. Rock wrens sing from sheltered gullies; mule deer quietly browse the green bushy banks of the Red Deer River that flows along the boundary of the park; the occasional golden eagle glides effortlessly overhead and the deep, liquid melody of the western meadowlark seems to follow you everywhere. And if you linger at the edge of the Red Deer, you will hear packs of coyotes howl to each other in evening communion, their calls and answers echoing across the badlands, enticing the listener to join in.

Of all the creatures that live on the prairies, perhaps the coyote has the right to be admired most—just for its unerring ability to survive! Early settlers, farmers and present-day ranchers have waged relentless war on these remarkably intelligent creatures. Coyotes have been poisoned, trapped, hunted and usually shot on sight, but still they manage to survive, boldly outwitting their two-legged predators. They are highly social animals, and without the wailing, lingering cry of the coyote that rolls across the plains at evening, symbolizing their freedom, the prairies would not be the same.

At sunset one evening, not far from Medicine Hat, we located an active coyote den tucked into the sheltering contours of a coulee. Crawling on our stomachs up an adjacent hill through tough grasses (and, inadvertently, over beds of prickly pear cactus), we reached the top where there was a clear view down to the den. Succumbing to some primitive instinct that lies deep in all of us, I threw back my head and rendered a high-pitched, ear-piercing coyote howl which I felt sure would draw everyone in the neighbourhood for miles around, ranchers as well as

△
As wind and water bite into ancient soils, strange hoodoo shapes emerge above eroded gullies in Dinosaur Park. The caps of harder shale will eventually fall as the soft sandstone continues to wear away.

△
The eternal symbol of drought. Tough little grasses cling to baked earth in southern Alberta's badlands.

▷
The mineralized bones of more than a hundred dinosaur skeletons have been dug up from the eroded valleys and ridges of Dinosaur Park. Today, no one is allowed to carry away fossils, and visitors to the park can still see dinosaur bones lying, literally, at their feet. This was once a salt water marsh at the edge of a vast inland sea, long before the Rocky Mountains emerged to the west.

coyotes. Moments later, four sets of very large ears followed by little furry heads popped over a ridge and four pairs of bright eyes gazed expectantly across in our direction — young coyotes looking for mother.

The cubs did not see us and loped on down the hill to the den, where they romped about while the sun went down. They were high-spirited and playful, conducting mock hunts through the tall grass and pouncing on each other from ambush. Both parents help raise the young and there is a great deal of affection expressed between members of the family. But coyotes are timid and shy in the presence of man (and with good reason). Every once in awhile one of the cubs would pause in his play and stare suspiciously in our direction.

As it darkened we began to wonder where the adults might be. Just as we were folding our tripods, John glanced over his shoulder and there was an adult, probably the mother, calmly sitting on her haunches two hills distant and carefully studying us. She looked as though she had been there for some time. When we made a slight movement in her direction, she lightly bounded away across the coulee ridge and out of sight. Three nights in a row we returned to the coulee but never saw the adult coyote again. It may be that she approached from downwind each time and picked up our scent well in advance. You cannot sneak up on a coyote — which undoubtedly helps to account for coyote longevity.

If the prairie is coyote country, it is also rattlesnake country. On a mid-June day we found ourselves high on sandy bluffs over the South Saskatchewan River looking for prairie rattlesnakes with John Gallimore, a high school biology teacher from Medicine Hat. These rattlers are descendants of reptiles that lived on the plains after the continental sea retreated millions of years ago. Over the centuries they have evolved and adapted to their changing environment. Some species disappeared completely but others, like the prairie rattlesnake, have survived and flourished, living on a diet of pocket gophers, deer mice, frogs and small birds, which they kill with poisonous venom and swallow whole.

Spring is not the safest time of year to go searching for rattlesnakes as they may be shedding their winter skins, a process which renders them partially blind and easily confused. Although we were assured that they never strike targets too large to swallow unless surprised or frightened, we conducted our search slowly and with maximum caution. Before long, a rattler was sighted, all three and a half feet of him slithering and gliding smoothly along the sandy bank. As we ap-

proached, the snake quickly disappeared into a cliffside crevice. John Gallimore, not in the least perturbed, knelt down and proceeded to dig out the hole, with his bare hands! Soon, a long, loud, steady buzzing sound issued from the depths. John reached in gingerly with the flattened end of a golf club and gently held down the snake's head in such a manner as not to injure it. Slipping his fingers behind the head, with its hinged fangs, he lifted the reptile quickly and harmlessly out of its hiding place.

The snake's body was well marked and coloured with shades of brown that blended into the prairie environment. I wrapped my fingers around its thick body and felt muscles rippling. The rattle—loosely jointed segments of dry skin at the end of the tail — buzzed and vibrated continuously. Like all reptiles, rattlesnakes are cold-blooded, but sensory pits located beside the nostrils allow them to detect heat from warm-blooded animals up to eighteen inches away, a fact we took well into consideration for our close-up photography.

Once released on the ground, the rattler coiled up into its moment-before-strike position, head cocked, black tongue flicking ominously, and buzzing tail straight up. As we walked around it, the snake coiled its body even more tightly and swivelled on the ground, always keeping us in a direct line of sight. We estimated his striking distance, and positioned ourselves with still cameras at what seemed to be a safe range. For filming, we mounted the 16mm Arriflex camera with a super wide-angle, "bug-eye" lens on the end of the tripod, and held camera and tripod out towards the snake like a long-handled vacuum cleaner. The snake unexpectedly jabbed at the camera, striking the lens with amazing speed and accuracy, and coating it with sticky venom. On the spot we all developed a healthy respect for rattlesnakes. Later, our film editor told us that the snake had struck the lens and returned to its coiled position in exactly twelve frames of film, or half a second.

Snakes have been greatly and unfairly maligned down through the ages. Certainly, the Bible's account didn't do the species any good. Like many other reptiles, including turtles and frogs, they are in need of sound conservation measures. But it is hard to make people responsive to the needs of cold-blooded reptiles which they either deeply fear or do not understand. On the plains of western Canada the relationship between rancher and prairie rattler is a wary co-existence.

From the high bluffs of the South Saskatchewan River the size of the prairies seems overwhelming. Sky, plain, roads and fenceposts race unhindered in all directions as far as the eye can see. There is a sensation of space, of freedom, and of

▷

A three foot prairie rattlesnake, coiled and ready to strike. Moments later, the camera was moved too close and the snake struck, spraying an expensive lens with venom that was extremely hard to remove.

ARRIFLEX

boundless exhilaration. The mind casts back easily to the early settlers who struggled westward during the late nineteenth century in search of a new life in a new land: pioneer farmers and homesteaders from Ontario and Quebec, lured on by the promise of free land grants on a newer, richer, agricultural frontier; British immigrants, some wealthy, but many less fortunate, fleeing the smoke and poverty of industrialized Britain; and American ranchers driving their cattle trains north with their dreams into the "last, best, west". Intensive immigration programs were launched at the turn of the century by the federal government. Poles, Russians, Germans, Ukrainians and Scandinavians — Clifford Sifton's "stalwart peasants in sheepskin jackets"—flooded into the prairie of western Canada, enticed away from the heart of Europe by persuasive government officials and the exaggerated promises of immigration posters.

The coming of the white man changed the face of the prairie. Settlers' ploughs broke the original sod, turning under native grasses that had long held down the plains and nourished the wildlife. Years later, the consequences were felt as winds rolled across the drought-filled "hungry thirties", sweeping up the precious prairie soil and carrying it away with a farmer's dreams.

Prairie fires, a terrifying but once natural pheonomenon, were now likely to be man-made, and more destructive. Settlers burned over the land to clear their homesteads; careless railway work gangs started brush fires that leapt out of control, and steam locomotives hissed fiery showers of sparks across the dry, hot plain. Range fires burned millions of acres of prairie and killed countless wild creatures.

Wildlife suffered most from the effects of western development and expansion. The buffalo, whose mighty herds had once filled the plain for as far as the eye could see, were gone forever from the prairie by the time the Canadian Pacific Railway was completed in 1885. A traveller who rode the steel tracks west in 1888 recorded in his diary:

> *All through today's journey, piled up at the leading stations along the road, were vast heaps of the bones of the earliest owners of the prairie — the buffalo. Giant heads and ribs and thigh bones, without one pick of meat on them, clean as a well-washed plate, white as driven snow, there they lay, a giant sacrifice on the altar of trade and civilization.*

The Indians at first refused to believe that the buffalo would never return and continued to search the plains, convinced they would reappear. Legend told them

△

The great buffalo herds were gone from the prairies by the 1880's, but you can still find their bones. These lie in a narrow coulee in Dinosaur Provincial Park, southern Alberta. The systematic shooting of the plains bison was the greatest wildlife slaughter in North American history.

◁

A few moments after dawn, on a high bank of the Red Deer River. The scene is not as idyllic as it looks — the air was thick with mosquitoes. Only the morning chorus of coyote families and songbirds broke the silence.

△
The story of one man's struggle to farm a dry land is laid out in almost chronological order on the prairie. Some of these rusting pieces of machinery were used through the dry years of the thirties. Each one brings back a memory to a man who stayed, and beat the drought. He is confident he could get this old tractor going again.

▷
An old tool shed in southern Alberta belonging to a farmer who hated to throw anything away. Wheel rims, fragments of harness, short pieces of chain, and old tools still hang from nails where they were carefully placed years ago. The drill on the right hand side still works perfectly.

that the buffalo had originally come from a great hole in the centre of a northern lake, and that when the white man arrived the herds had gone back into that lake, from where they would eventually re-emerge.

Pronghorn antelope almost suffered a fate similar to that of the buffalo. After the great bison herds had gone from the prairies, hunters and hard winters combined to take a toll of the pronghorn. But antelope are so well adapted to their flat, prairie environment that they were able to survive. The fastest, fleetest creatures on the plains, they can bound effortlessly over the grasslands at forty miles per hour and sometimes reach fifty to sixty miles per hour in short, sudden bursts. They are trim and graceful members of the deer family, beautifully marked in shades of creamy white and tan. The prairie is indeed enriched by the presence of such charming creatures. But, like the coyote, they have much to fear from man. There is still an annual hunting season conducted under special permit.

With an intelligence born to all creatures that live in exposed places, pronghorn have learned that the safest place on the plain is often amongst cattle. There you will find them, particularly during hunting season, white rumps showing up clearly in the distance, peacefully grazing with a rancher's herds on the open prairie.

Ranching in southern Alberta's short grass country has never been easy. Summers are hot, and punctuated with erratic and often violent thunderstorms that turn dusty sideroads into impassable quagmires of mud and clay. Tornadoes may twist suddenly from a wall of black storm clouds, assaulting the land without warning. Drought is far more regular and persistent, and can last for months, or even years.

It took courage to settle this land and determination to stay. Many a plough that broke the sod also broke the sodbuster in the dry, windy thirties. Families left the west in droves during the Depression years. Some mortgaged their farms and headed back east; others simply abandoned the land, defeated by drought, depression and black clouds of grasshoppers that stripped bare both the land and their future. But not all left. Talk to ranchers who stayed, who endured, and they will tell you there was no rain for twelve years, that their stock died of thirst and starvation on the range, and that they had to sell calves because there was no money for feed.

One rancher southwest of Medicine Hat told us that he had only three cows and twenty sheep in 1936. "Sold two calves at $2.50 apiece that year", he said; "sold them so's they wouldn't die on me". He remembers the hot winds that drove prairie

sand up through the floorboards each day, piling it up five inches deep in his kitchen. And it was hot—115° one morning at six o'clock. "If you dropped a crowbar for twenty minutes on the plain, you couldn't pick it up again, it was that hot". He chuckled. In a three room cabin, he and his wife raised five children and stuck it out. He is still there, alone now, ranching his two sections of land with care, respect and a lot of love, as he has always done. We asked him about drought. Pushing back his old felt hat, he looked up at the hot sky and, with a sense of humour that saved many a rancher in the Depression, replied: "Well now . . . we had a few good showers in the sixties. We should be coming up for some more rain in a couple of years."

It may be a dry land, but all across the Canadian prairie the abundance of bird life is astonishing. These plains have been called the "duck factory" of North America, for almost eighty percent of all the continent's ducks nest and breed in southern Alberta, Saskatchewan and Manitoba. In the spring and fall you will see multitudes of waterfowl on their annual migrations, wheeling down to familiar prairie potholes, ponds, tiny lakes and sloughs — those small depressions in the land that catch and hold the vital spring runoff and rainfall. Sloughs are like desert oases for waterfowl. They are rich in aquatic plants and their tall cat-tails make well concealed nesting sites. During a wet spring literally millions of these precious sloughs are reflected across Canada's prairie provinces.

On one unforgettable evening we walked to the edge of a prairie slough and marvelled at the life that water brings to a dry country. White faced cattle browsed a few yards away from three coyotes that were busily hunting ground squirrels in the tall grass and sagebrush. A few antelope slipped in among the cattle, and a flock of some thirty Canada geese, anxiously watching the coyotes, were lined up on the bank. Overhead, string after string of mallards and pintails passed across the sky, catching a red glow from the west and spiralling down to unseen ponds behind the contours of a gently rolling landscape. It was a perfect image of the unexpected abundance of wildlife that flourishes on a seemingly arid land.

It is these unexpected elements that make a trip into the prairie so fascinating. Every sideroad has its rewards, and every hike among the coulees or over the plain strengthens your impression of space and freedom. If wildlife seems unusually visible it may simply be that here you can see farther and more clearly than in parts of

◁
First touches of snow in the foothills of the Rockies, near Nanton, Alberta. This is a particularly beautiful area when the poplars are turning gold in late September.

Canada where horizons are limited by mountains, hills and tall trees. Only the traveller who takes the time to explore instead of racing across the prairie at 60mph, will understand and share these impressions of a big and vital land. Forget the old myth about the "dry, arid, empty" plain. Keep your eyes, ears, and mind open and you will soon discover how full, how varied, and how utterly splendid this land really is.

1▽

2∇

3▽
4▷

5◁

6▷
7▷

8▽

Algonquin: A Place For All Seasons

To some of us the word itself
is an expression of emotion,
a word that evokes priceless memories:
the fragrance of campfire smoke,
the squeak of snowshoes at thirty below,
the golden mists of September steaming
under the bow of a silent canoe.

Spring comes reluctantly to Ontario, and the northwest winds carry the echoes of winter well into May. There is no sudden blaze of flowers or bursting of leaves, but a slow awakening, tempered by cool nights and soils that stubbornly refuse to warm up. In the country, the farmer who gets his corn in before May 24 stores the planter away in the machine shed with relief. Then June arrives, and suddenly it is summer.

Every spring we wait impatiently through the first weeks of April as the blue ice of winter slowly darkens, melting away from the shorelines until the wind finds a toe-hold on the open water and finishes the job. Now the rituals of spring begin. The canoe comes home from a dusty barn where it has spent the winter, its wounded canvas once more repaired and painted, its gunwales and ribs sanded and gleaming with new varnish. Packs are taken out and shaken, disgorging such treasures as old pieces of rope, a missing knife, some ancient bouillon cubes. Tattered maps are

△
A summer storm rolls across Algonquin in a dramatic play of light and dark above the pines. Watching storms as they gather and mature is a fascinating experience, and there is nothing quite like the sound of rain on the roof of a well pitched tent in the wilderness.

△
For many wilderness travellers, loons symbolize everything that is wild and free. One Canadian writer has described their call as "woman wailing for her demon lover". The variety and purity of their calls are beautiful beyond description.

spread out once more on the living room carpet, and the mind eagerly wanders among the contours and twisting blue lines, converting these familiar symbols into cliffs and streams, or beaver dams and portages best forgotten. An old box of freeze-dried food reappears, and the merits of chicken sawdust stew and cardboard beef are once more discussed. A trusted check-list of equipment and food is ticked off, item by item, until the packs will take no more, and it's time to start whittling away at the gear you really don't need. At last the first weekend in May approaches and you begin to watch the weather systems, remembering how unspeakably cold it was last year, or the time it rained for four days and turned to snow on the fifth.

Every year it is just as cold. But there is pure magic in that first moment as you push away from shore. The canoe seems to hang suspended above the dark water, momentarily floating in space, quietly separating from the land that has held you through the winter months. And now the noise and tumult and vibrations of the city 200 miles away begin to fade. A bird sings, a breeze touches the water, and a profound silence hangs over the forest. You lay the paddles quietly across the gunwales and drift, listening, as your tensions slip gently away into that silence.

Later, lying on the cold granite rock beside a warm fire and staring up at the stars that promise frost before morning, you hear the first territorial cries of loons, far down the lake. You hear them again from the fluffy warmth of your sleeping bag, and again in your sleep as they call far into the night. There is no greater peace than the first night of the first canoe trip in spring.

With the first portage comes a kind of fierce exuberance, a physical joy, as the heart pumps blood to straining shoulders and aching legs, and the cold clean air fills your lungs. The separation from civilization continues to widen as you push deeper into the woods, down streams barricaded by beavers, and on across the lakes and secret places unfolding before your canoe.

There is a place in this land called Algonquin. On the map of Ontario it is a large, irregularly shaped area north of the rough and rocky farmlands that cling to the rising contours of the Canadian Shield. Within its shaded green boundaries is a marvellous, rugged piece of country, where a wild tangle of lakes, rivers, streams and precambrian rock lies among great hardwood hills and dark fringes of pines and spruce.

Algonquin. To some of us the word itself is an expression of emotion, a word that evokes priceless memories: the fragrance of campfire smoke, the squeak of snowshoes at 30° below, the golden mists of September steaming under the silent bow of a canoe. Such is the stuff of wilderness. When you consider that Algonquin covers 3,000 square miles, contains some 2,000 lakes and the headwaters of five major rivers, and can be reached easily within three and a half hours from Toronto, you begin to understand the immense value of this great park. On a continent where highways and tall buildings are considered a mark of progress, the survival of Algonquin is, indeed, a miracle. What protects Algonquin is its sheer size. Commercial lumbering and haphazard planning have brought great pressure on the park's wilderness qualities, but anyone who can read a map can still have a satisfying wilderness experience there.

Our own love affair with Algonquin began in 1965 during production of a television film. Since then we have spent every spare moment hiking through its lakes and trails and portages.

In 1969 we celebrated a week of our honeymoon on a canoe trip down the Crow River. Early one morning, at the entrance to the river, an adult timber wolf walked slowly through our camp, staring briefly at us with great grey eyes from less than thirty feet away, and then disappearing like smoke. For us this visitation was somehow an honour, a reminder that timber wolves run free here, and that this is one of the few places on earth where you might hear them howl their joyous song of freedom.

In the fall of 1970 we chose one of those canoe routes "that you can't get to from here", and battled in through a dozen overgrown portages, an endless series of beaver dams and uncounted fallen trees to the shallow end of the Nipissing River. There the river was nothing more than a stream, the water was low and the mud deep, and much of the time we were pulling or pushing the canoe through a soggy jungle of tag alders. But every obstacle passed was another psychological barrier between us and the city we had left behind, and the photographic and spiritual rewards were remarkable.

On the third day we were camped on rising ground overlooking a rich marsh and the winding channel of the Nipissing. During the night we had heard wolves howling and barking a few miles away but had been too lazy to get up and howl back. However, we were out in the marsh before sunrise, paddling among the frosted grasses and jewelled cobwebs that slipped quietly past us in the mist. It was one of Algonquin's perfect, classic September mornings, and became so wildly

△
Deep in Algonquin's interior the Crow River flows dark and cool. Algonquin was established as a park in 1893, after most of the surrounding area had been heavily logged. One reason for creating the park was to protect the headwaters of five major rivers.

△
A curious garter snake, probably just emerging from hibernation, examines the camera that has been taking its picture. We spent more than an hour here, moving very quietly as the snakes slithered around us, apparently becoming accustomed to our cameras.

beautiful that we shot more than 200 pictures before breakfast.

Moments before the sun cleared the pines and turned the mist from grey to gold, Janet quietly shipped her paddle and whispered: "Why don't you try a wolf howl?" My efforts broke the silence to echo among the hills. Seconds later the answer came. From the south, only a few hundred yards away, a family responded, the pups yipping and yelping beside the adults. From the east came a single howl. From the west, two adults joined in, lending their voices to this incredible dawn chorus. We could hardly speak. Just half an hour later, as the stern of the canoe brushed against a curve in the stream called Loontail Creek, a grey, bushy tail rose briefly about ten feet away. I grabbed the bank with one hand, a camera with the other, and jumped out. Again, like smoke, he was gone, but Janet spotted him dodging away among the trees. It is moments like this that nourish the passions for Algonquin.

We have found that these experiences can be greatly enhanced by a love of photography. All at once your goals become very clear. Every season holds a promise, and you develop a hunger for travelling deeper and deeper into wilderness, to visit the most remote area you possibly can. This is not the atavistic desire of the hunter, but the urge to capture and record moments of time in a wild land beyond the sight and experience of most people. The only limit to wilderness photography is one's own creativity.

Often it is the camera that leads the photographer, revealing subtle blends of colour and form among the patterns of nature, isolating tiny moments of intense beauty that the eye could not see nor the mind anticipate. But you learn; you learn when to search with a macro lens, and when to stand back like a sniper, probing the wilderness with a telephoto eye. And you learn that wilderness photography is anticipation — being at the right place at the right moment.

Autumn in Algonquin brings many of those moments. As September slips away, the leaves blaze briefly in a final celebration of colour, painting the hills with fire that must eventually die under the onslaught of October winds and driving rain. Then the forest grows quiet, and the land seems to wait for winter. By November most of the migrant birds are gone. Only the occasional loon or merganser fishes in the lakes, and the tough little birds who will stay and face the winter are gathering into groups. Siskins, goldfinches, grosbeaks and crossbills twitter among seed bearing trees, scattering empty hulls in a gentle shower of chaff. Chickadees flit through the lower levels like wind-driven leaves, peering excitedly under fragments of bark, walking upside down, extracting insect eggs and other treasures from tiny crevices. Then comes the snow, and quick cold spells that begin to lock up the lakes. By Christmas the park is white and silent. But still the real winter has not arrived.

Winter in Algonquin is the blazing whiteness and crackling temperatures of February, with deep, dry snow and lakes frozen like super-cooled steel. Winter is wolf tracks, long blue shadows, and the orange after-glow of the western sky among the first bright stars of evening. It is the lake ice that rumbles like thunder in the night as the cold grows more intense, until the hardwood fibres begin to join in, snapping and booming like distant gunfire in the forest. "Would you like to come with us tonight?" a naturalist once asked. "We're going out to listen to the hardwoods pop."

Winter is the burning cold of your sleeping bag as the first tentative foot goes in, and the frost that was once your breath freezes on your pillow, or hangs in soft white formations from the tent roof above. It is the white smoke of a breakfast fire rising through the snow like steam, and the "whiskey-jacks", fluffed up to an impossible size, that arrive at the precise moment you open a loaf of bread.

You strap on your snowshoes and turn into the brilliance of a cold sun that seems to have taken its warmth and gone south for the winter. But the sudden chill that shivered into your bones as you threw snow on the fire is quickly gone as thigh muscles pump against the familiar weight of snowshoes in the deep, dry snow. At once you are too warm, and parkas snap open to let the body breathe. Above you the Canada jays that shared your breakfast prepare to follow and share your lunch. By the end of the day they will have stored little fragments of your sandwiches in trees all along the trail. You rest for a moment in silence, and contemplate these 3,000 square miles of peace — this oasis of calm in a land gone mad with snowmobiles.

The winter! the brightness that blinds you,
The white land locked tight as a drum,
The cold fear that follows and finds you,
The silence that bludgeons you dumb.
The snows that are older than history,
The woods where the weird shadows slant;
The stillness, the moonlight, the mystery,
I've bade 'em good-bye—but I can't.

△
One of Algonquin's most lively, visible and vocal creatures, a red squirrel. Canoeists are frequently met at their chosen campsites by the scolding of these little creatures, and late fall campers sometimes have to endure a rain of sticky pine cones as the squirrel gathers a supply of food.

△
Racoons are usually nocturnal, and spend the daylight hours sleeping. This one was hungry after a long cold spell and climbed down to investigate the irresistible smell of brown bread. Although completely wild, he accepted food from our fingers and then returned to his comfortable perch.

▷
The soft light of a winter morning early in January. These stretches of open water are excellent places to watch for otter and beaver activity.

Robert Service was speaking of a Yukon winter, but his words could equally well describe Algonquin in February. The slowly returning sun has a special brilliance as it nudges higher into the southern sky and turns every snow-swept lake into a blinding reflector, contrasting a sea of white light against the deep blue reaches of the northern hemisphere. Temperatures plunge with the sunset, and darkness brings a glittering canopy of constellations that seem to rest on the black spires of pine trees. Sometimes, ten perfect days will pass before the wind swings to the southwest to bring moist air and swirling storms.

It was during one of those still, sparkling periods of deep cold that we first spent a night with the snow beneath us and only thin cotton above. With a good friend to guide us, we made camp in the drifted snow at the edge of a frozen marsh. The friend was Bill Mason, perhaps the finest wilderness film maker in Canada—a man who waits for winter with the same anticipation most people reserve for summer.

Sitting over a campfire that tried to take the edge off temperatures falling to 44° below, we exchanged long and eloquent periods of silence. Conversation can be an intrusion in moments of peace. However, one interruption was hard to believe. As the fire melted a circle of snow and began nibbling at the mosses, a tiny black insect crawled away from the heat. It was the old scourge of the north, a blackfly. We examined its familiar silhouette, anticipating the biting swarms that would claim this marsh in the spring. Biologists told us later that it could not have been a blackfly, that this species winters in the egg stage only. We decided to live with our convictions, perhaps sharing with northerners the belief that blackflies never really die—they just burrow under the snow and wait for early tourists!

By midnight the fire was only a wisp of steam in the snow. We were in our tents, deep in the down-filled comfort of arctic sleeping bags, and separated from the packed snow beneath by two inches of foam rubber. The cold had slipped quietly into the tents behind us and every breath produced a thickening layer of frost at the rim of each bag. Above us, fluffy white chrystals formed delicate patterns on the roof, hanging briefly like stalactites in a cave and then falling softly onto our faces. We managed to burrow deep enough to stay warm, breathing through a careful arrangement of folded cloth. It was a good experience, slightly tempered by the shock of dressing in the paralyzing cold of dawn.

Breakfast was the sizzle of bacon, a parade of Canada jays, a column of white smoke in the still morning air, and long yellow rays of light touching the marsh.

△
Smoke Lake at thirty below zero on a clear February morning. An earlier thaw had melted away snow and slush on the ice surface, and the return of cold weather turned Algonquin's two thousand lakes into shining steel.

▷
Spring ice formations at the edge of an Algonquin stream. The stream carries melt-water from the forest, and superb ice patterns are produced by spray and droplets during a cold night.

Later, searching for dry wood in deep snow beside a hollow tree, we disturbed a flying squirrel who then made an unusual daylight appearance, his round black eyes shining in the sunlight. He climbed far above us and kicked off into space, soaring over fifty feet, like a furry, grey handkerchief with legs at each corner. As he reached the end of his glide he swooped sharply upwards and landed like a feather on the trunk of a pine. It was a beautiful display by one of Algonquin's most delightful creatures.

We snowshoed away from the marsh that had given us twenty-four hours of memories, pulling our heavy toboggan over a portage trail used by canoeists in the summer—a reminder that in just over two months the lakes would once again be open, and the toboggan would change places with the canoe. Algonquin is indeed a place for all seasons.

If some of us become emotional about our Algonquins it is because we need these escape routes from the subtle pressures and self-inflicted tensions that simmer within our souls. For some, a busy campground with electricity and running water is enough. So be it. If our wilderness is to survive it is essential that not all of us jam into it at once.

Aldo Leopold once wrote: "Wilderness is a resource which can shrink, but not grow". Those words should be burned into the office doors of all Resource Ministers in Canada. Every road that snakes into the interior of a park, every campground that expands, every timber license that is renewed, every mineral deposit that is exploited is an erosion of the very wilderness quality that draws people to that park.

Like many North American parks, Algonquin has been studied, planned criticized and loved with varying degrees of urgency and emotion for many years. Too many parks are now managed under the concept of "multiple use", an unfortunate and all-embracing description that permits commercial activities such as logging to last forever. Perhaps some day we will persuade governments to stop trying to make money out of parks, and to pay more attention to sound planning principles instead. In a place like Algonquin the presence of trucks and chain saws is a perpetual irritant and a most incompatible land use in such a vitally important park.

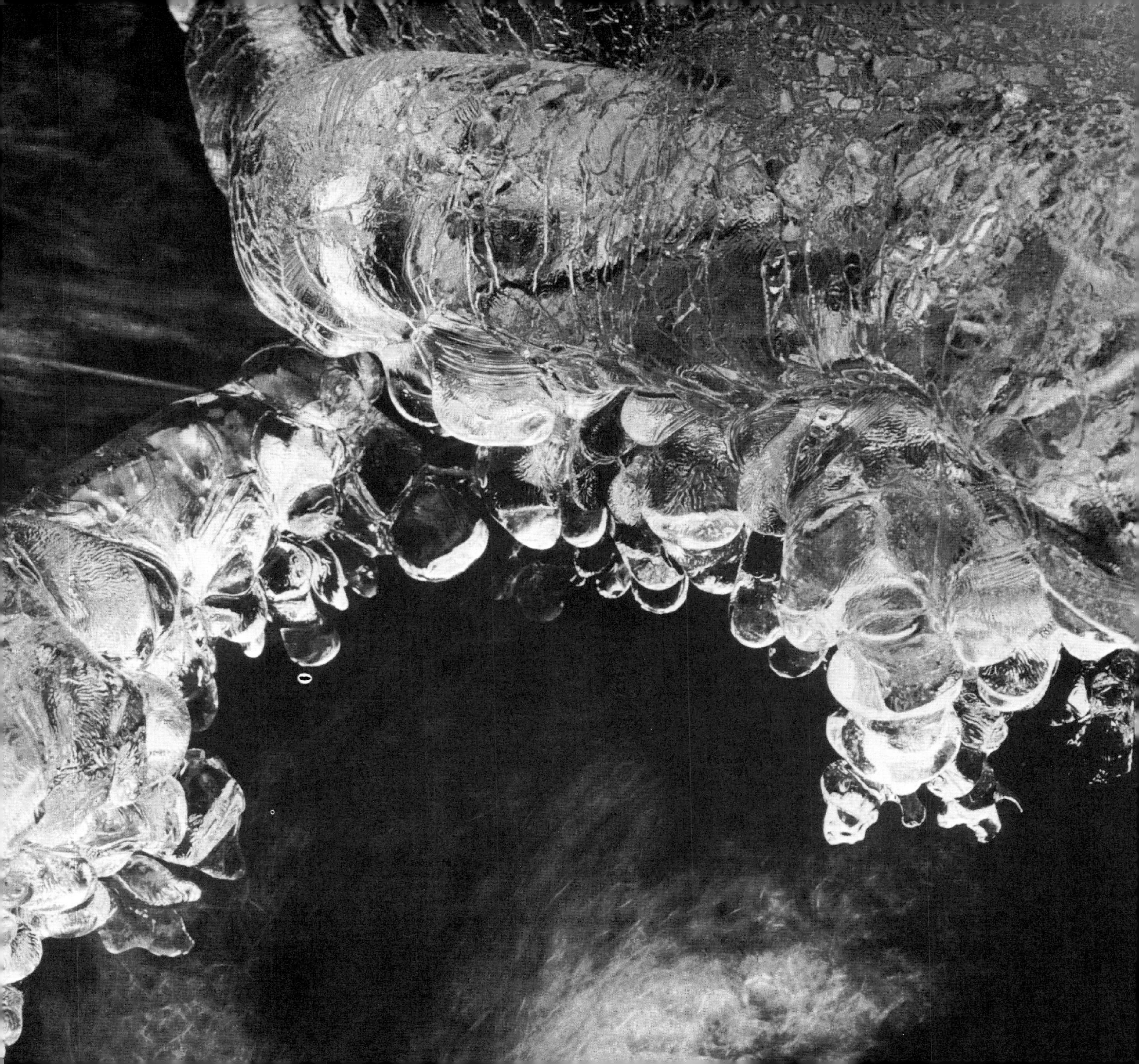

△
Canada jays, or "Whiskey-jacks", are frequent and delightful companions on snowshoeing trips. They have a compulsion to find and store food in the winter, and their only real interest in man is the food that he carries.

Ironically, the most immediate threat to North America's parks is the people who use them in ever increasing numbers. It is neither possible nor sensible to attempt to satisfy everyone's needs on the same piece of ground. Only by wise and determined planning will these places be saved for those generations which will need wild space so desperately in the future.

Somehow Algonquin survives the onslaught of our most uncivilized civilization. Like a fine old cathedral that stands above the rubble of a bulldozer economy, the park continues to exist, to give visitors a glimpse of the past and to offer those who are willing to work for it a priceless wilderness experience just a few hours away from millions of people. But, like freedom, the price of wilderness is eternal vigilance. It is time to leave Algonquin alone, to let the natural rhythms and forces of wilderness flow unassisted by chain saws or trucks. Let the wildfire burn where it must. Let the old trees die where they stand and become nature's apartment houses for tiny creatures. Let those who would see the wild interior take their paddles and their snowshoes along the trails of the Algonkian Indians, and know the satisfaction of working for their wilderness. Let no man make a dollar from the soil of this public land. Let Algonquin grow old and wild for future generations. Let it be.

1◁
2▽

3▽

4▽

5▽

6▽

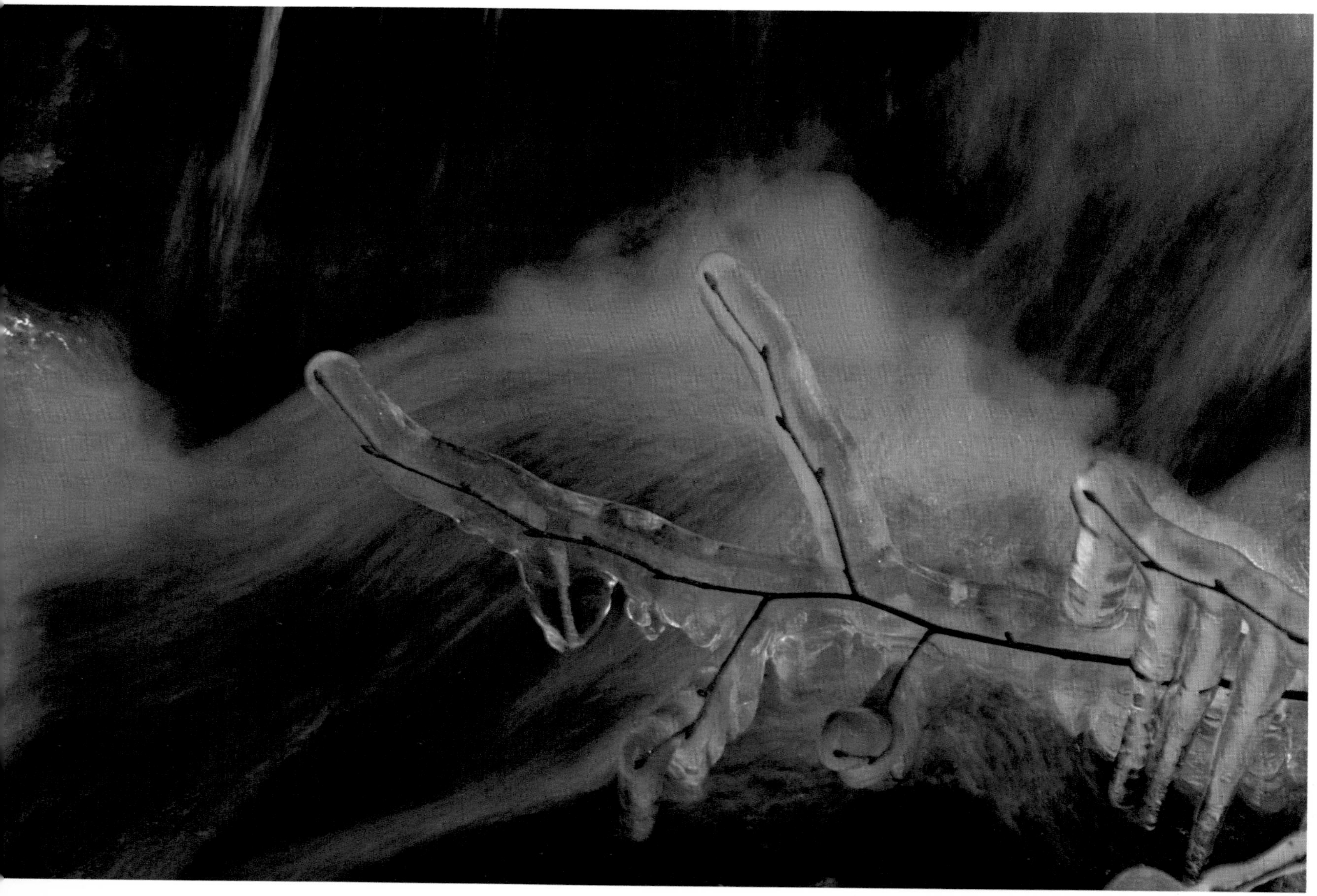

7▽

8▷

Land Of The St. Lawrence

Standing high on the cliffs of Forillon,
you can see the occasional seal bobbing about
in the waves below
or, if you are lucky, whales feeding
in the currents of the St. Lawrence.
Almost certainly you will see long strings of white gannets
streaming past the headland cliffs
to Bonaventure Island.

Clouds of great white birds descend like snowflakes, drifting and swirling in on the cold winds of early May and lining the shoreline between Quebec City and Cap Tourmente. They come with the first touches of spring to the St. Lawrence, spilling wind over wings in graceful descent patterns, their pure white forms relieving the harshness of a still wintry landscape. On the tidal flats and marshes of the river they furrow the muddy soil with anxious bills in search of tasty plant roots and gabble together in loud, welcoming chorus. The greater snow geese are returning once more to Cap Tourmente, their traditional resting place en route to nesting grounds 2,000 miles away in the high Arctic.

△
A gannet, magnificent in flight, approaches the nesting colony on Bonaventure Island.

Greater snow geese come twice a year to Cap Tourmente: in the spring on their northward migration, and again in the autumn as they head south with their new families. Their latin name, *hyperborea*, means "from beyond the north wind" and, like the words of the song, they "come with the spring and they're gone with the wind". Migrations such as this whisper of age and tradition. Four hundred years ago weather-beaten sailing ships found their way far inland from the sea for the first time, and passed under this same brooding headland cliff of Cap Tourmente, a silent sentinel above the great river that has drawn men deep into the heart of the continent. Early explorers might well have been greeted by the ancestors of these greater snow geese that cluster on the shoreline of Cap Tourmente, graceful continental migrants, annual visitors to the land of the St. Lawrence.

The land of the St. Lawrence is old. It has experienced great battles of geological forces that scoured, wrenched and changed the landscape. It has felt the full tide of human history as French and English fought for control of the St. Lawrence river system, a trade and transportation route that stretched halfway across the continent and shaped the destiny of a northern commercial empire. It is the oldest settled region in Canada, yet a journey through the land of the St. Lawrence is today still a journey of discovery, of unexpected surprises—of elusive caribou, browsing moose, noisy seabird colonies, awesome fiords, rugged mountains contrasting with gentle lowlands, and whales that return each summer to the protected waters of a living Gulf.

East of Quebec City the river begins to widen, as salt water from the Atlantic meets fresh water flowing out from the centre of the continent. Along both shores the cool winds of July blow across fields blanketed with daisies and buttercups, sweeping down to the river. Drive the north shore and these meadows soon give way to rolling forested hills, dense bush, rock and tumbling rivers, for this is the southern edge of the great Canadian Shield. But drive the south shore to the Gaspé Peninsula, and you will discover a land that seems more gentle. The coastal road winds past farms rolling to the river in the characteristic narrow strips of the old seigneurial system, and through tiny villages and towns tucked into valleys and lowlands. In the Gaspé, deep in the heart of rural French Canada, you can still find families that work the fields together, milk cows by the roadside in the late afternoon light, and ridge potato fields with horses in the old, time-proven way. Sometimes it seems as though life has changed little in the Gaspé. It conveys a sense of permanence, timelessness and history not found anywhere else in Canada.

△

Milking time on the north shore of the St. Lawrence. In this age of agribusiness and elaborate milking parlours, it is rare, indeed, to find a family milking their cows in an open field.

▷

A few miles east of Quebec City thousands of greater snow geese fill the marshes and mud flats of the St. Lawrence every spring, before continuing on their northward migration to high Arctic islands. They will stay here for about six weeks and pass through again in the fall on their way south.

This image of the Gaspé is abruptly changed if you turn away from the St. Lawrence midway down the peninsula and head inland towards Gaspesian Park in the Chic Choc Mountains, at the edge of the Appalachian Mountain range. Few people realize that some of the highest accessible peaks in eastern Canada are in this area of southern Quebec. One of them, Mont Jacques Cartier, rises to a height of 4,300 feet. High on its tundra plateau is a tiny herd of woodland caribou, survivor of the herds that were once hunted almost to extinction in past centuries. The park was set aside in 1937 to preserve the animals but no one knows how many inhabit the windswept mountain tops. Some believe there are as many as 500 caribou, but others fear there are fewer than forty. It is a difficult trek up the Chic Chocs and the caribou have few two-legged visitors.

Gaspesian Park shares a common boundary with Matane Provincial Park and as you drive the rough old roads that link them you glimpse a landscape sometimes reminiscent of the Yukon Territory. Broad, clean rivers flow across gravel bars, their banks lined with tall spruce trees leaning over the water. Steeply wooded slopes rise and disappear into the morning mist, suggesting great mountains far above. The Chic Choc Mountains are smaller and more rounded than those in the Yukon, but the snow patches trapped in gullies beyond the tree line linger far into the summer, and the sub-artic conditions on the heights are real enough. As if to complete the illusion, moose splash out from the edges of spruce bogs and wade into deep water to graze on aquatic vegetation.

Matane Provincial Park is famous for moose. Indeed, the Park Superintendent told us that one lake in particular, L'Étang à la truite, has a concentration of moose greater than that found anywhere else in Quebec. In most parts of Canada moose are shy of man. One's first sight of these large creatures is often a hurried glimpse as they melt into the trees at the first hint of your presence. They are the largest members of the deer family, and with their long legs and elongated snouts are splendidly adapted to a marshy environment. Summer mornings and evenings are spent browsing in swamps and shallow lakes, grazing on thick vegetation under the water's surface. They wade out after aquatic plants and often submerge themselves completely. There is even a record of a moose diving to a depth of eighteen feet and remaining submerged for more than thirty seconds.

In Matane there is an unusual mineral spring. Known as "le vasière", it is a small, muddy pond about seventy-five feet wide. A network of beaten trails that lead from all directions through the woods to the pond gives evidence that, for some

△
A groundhog enjoying the benefits of home ownership near Cap Tourmente. His tunnels emerge inside the mud floor of this abandoned cabin. Groundhogs have proved remarkably adaptable and resilient in the face of urban expansion and sharpshooting farm boys.

▷
The edge of a salt water marsh beneath the densely wooded hills of Forillon National Park, Quebec.

△
This young bull moose was so thoroughly captivated by the mineral waters of a vasière *in Matane Provincial Park, Quebec, that he knelt down in order to drink in comfort from the shallow spring. No one could explain the properties of this spring and there was no apparent salty flavour.*

reason, moose are strangely attracted to these muddy waters. Early one morning we crept through the woods to the *vasière* and found a young bull moose contentedly lapping at the clear trickle where the mineralized waters emerged from the ground. Apparently oblivious to our silent arrival, and only dimly aware of the camera eagerly whirring in the bushes, he seemed to be well and truly hooked on the unique mineral qualities of the spring. Suddenly, he collapsed his long front legs and knelt down to drink. It was a remarkable sight!

The moose shared a common misery with us. It was at the height of Quebec's fly season and his big ears flopped back and forth in a vain attempt to ward off battalions of mosquitos, blackflies and deerflies which stormed around his head. We also noticed, with a great deal of amusement, that every few minutes the moose was compelled to relieve himself (all that salty water!), a business that took quite some time. The mineralized water must have been travelling right through him almost in a matter of minutes. John later went upstream and tasted the water where it emerged clear and pure from the ground, but could detect no unusual flavour. The moose was obviously enjoying something in the *vasière* waters and whatever it was we were grateful, for it allowed us to obtain some most unusual film and photographs.

Eighty miles east of Matane the Gaspé Peninsula comes to an abrupt end. Out on the very tip, the headland cliffs of Forillon National Park rise in a great, grey, sloping block from the sea and tower to a height of 600 feet. Colonies of cormorants nest there on narrow ledges, and far below tides wash in to sheltered bays, hidden coves, and cobble beaches that you can find only at low tide. Standing high on the cliffs of Forillon, you can see the occasional seal bobbing about in the waves below, or, if you are lucky, whales swimming and feeding in the currents of the St. Lawrence. Almost certainly you will see long strings of white gannets streaming past the headland cliffs to Bonaventure Island, thirty miles to the south across the Gulf waters.

The bird colonies of Bonaventure Island and neighbouring Percé Rock have been described as the most spectacular ornithological sight on the North American continent. Bonaventure lies just three miles off the village of Percé on the east coast of the Gaspé Peninsula, and has long been a mecca for tourists, birdwatchers, ornithologists and wildlife photographers. Cormorants, great black-backed gulls, herring gulls, kittiwakes, guillemots, razorbill auks, common murres, puffins and petrels are among the many thousands of seabirds that nest on the red sandstone ledges and high cliffs of Bonaventure. But the island's most famous residents are the beautiful white gannets, birds that now number close to 50,000 in the colony.

Adult gannets are superb subjects for the camera, with their distinctive cheek markings, blue-rimmed eyes, and a wing span of over six feet. They are awkward on land but possess a singular beauty and grace of movement in flight, and we delighted in filming them in slow motion.

The birds begin to arrive at the colony in April, each mated pair returning to the same location, sometimes even to the same nest, as the previous year. Territories are roughly defined by the distance each bird can peck while sitting on the nest. Thousands crowd the colony, all shrieking their raucous calls and loudly defending their nesting sites. How an adult can recognize its own tiny territory remains a mystery. Each time one returns to the nest it is greeted by its mate in an elaborate ritual of rubbing necks and tapping bills.

The gannets of Bonaventure are well protected now, but it was not always so. Their very survival was once in grave doubt. For early settlers in Canada the presence of bird colonies was a blessing. Norman and Breton fishermen in the sixteenth century used birds for bait, and after the arrival of permanent French settlement in the region the birds also provided fresh meat and eggs. Excessive exploitation quickly brought a rapid decline in the seabird populations.

John James Audubon voyaged into the St. Lawrence Gulf in 1833 and witnessed the reckless slaughter of bird species. He reported that commercial "eggers" took every egg they could collect, forcing the birds to lay fresh: "by robbing them regularly they compel them to lay until nature is exhausted, but so few young are raised". Egging was profitable business in the nineteenth century and Audubon related how one party of four men took 40,000 eggs over a two month period, selling them in Halifax for twenty-five cents a dozen. "These wonderful nurseries must be finally destroyed", Audubon wrote, "unless some kind government interpose to put a stop to all this shameful destruction."

The egging and killing continued, however. Canadian ornithologist, Percy Taverner visited the bird colonies in 1914 and was appalled by the scene of devastation that greeted his eyes on Bonaventure. Boatloads of sportsmen had shot up the rookeries, littering the island's rocky base with the bodies of dead and dying birds, their "sodden remains washed back and forth in the adjoining sea". Saddest of all, reported Taverner, was the scene on the lower ledges of the cliffs where pot shots

△
One of the themes being stressed in Forillon National Park is the traditional relationship between man, the land and the sea. This fishing wharf remains active within the park, and Gaspé fishermen use it daily.

△
Like highrise dwellers in a city, the birds of Bonaventure Island occupy neatly defined territories on sheer rock cliffs above the sea. This sanctuary is one of the great attractions of the Gaspé Peninsula and is constantly circled by tour boats during the summer.

had been aimed into the sitting birds:

> *Here for some distance lay a trail of dead birds still on the nests where they had been shot, with the young pinned beneath the cold bodies of their parents. Other young stood disconsolately about until a humane heel or blow from the gunstock put an end to their hunger and cold.*
>
> *Below, on the rocks just above the swirl of the sea where they had managed to clamber, were numerous wounded adults patiently awaiting death that lingered in its coming.*

The colonies were finally protected in 1919 when the ledges of Bonaventure Island and Percé Rock were declared bird sanctuaries by the Quebec and federal governments. The years of senseless slaughter had ended. Today, boatloads of photographers replace the earlier boatloads of hunters. The Canadian Wildlife Service has carefully laid out trails a safe distance from the nesting areas and maintains a watchful eye of the gannet population. Any disturbance during incubation can be critical to a bird that lays only one egg.

Late in July we crossed the St. Lawrence and drove back along the north shore to Tadoussac, at the rocky entrance to the Saguenay River. We were searchig for whales. Each summer numerous whale species move inland from the Atlantic, swimming along the north shore of the St. Lawrence to where the cold Gulf waters sweep against the subterranean ledge of the Saguenay and the mixture combines to produce a marine environment rich in nutrients. Fin whales, sei, minke, beluga, humpback, and even great blue whales move into this region during the summer months to feed on plankton, schools of shrimp and capelin that flourish in the cold waters. Whale-watching has become an increasingly popular sport, and it is a splendid sight, indeed, to see these magnificent creatures of the sea return each year to the protected waters of the Gulf.

Of all the whales that return to the St. Lawrence, the beluga are the most beautiful. Travelling in groups, they flow and porpoise through the water in a graceful harmony and unity of fluid motion, their snow-white forms gliding, dipping, disappearing and rising again through the crested waves. They are small whales, about fifteen feet in length. Beluga seldom dive deep but can stay submerged for ten to fifteen minutes, surfacing each time a considerable distance away from where they went down. Filming them was difficult, for only guesswork told us where they might come up.

Late one afternoon John sighted a vapour curtain hanging momentarily in the air marking the spot where a whale had surfaced to blow and draw new breath. Our vessel approached and as the whale rose again we all heard the blow, like a great sigh across the waters. It was a finback, second only to the giant blue in size. We were reminded again that whale-watching is much like watching icebergs—you see only the tip. When you are looking at the small portion of whale that breaks the surface, it is hard to believe there may be another seventy feet underwater.

With the coming of autumn, the many whale species that frequent the protected waters of the Gulf will begin their long migratory journey back along the rugged north shore and out to the Atlantic from whence they came. An uncertain future awaits them there. International exploitation of declining whale species has not stopped in spite of pleas for conservation by concerned citizens and efforts by the International Whaling Commission. Humpback, minke, and right whale populations have all been seriously depleted, and the blue whale has been hunted so heavily throughout the world that surviving numbers are reportedly now in the mere hundreds. Unless protected, many of their species will pass into extinction in our lifetime. A ten-year moratorium on all commercial whaling was proposed in 1973 by the International Whaling Commission. The proposal was defeated. Having seen and filmed the beautiful whales of the St. Lawrence, we can only hope that reason and compassion will rule the affairs of men, and that each year these gentle and marvellously intelligent creatures will be permitted to return, unmolested, to the protected waters of the Gulf.

Watching the largest living creatures on earth swim past granite cliffs whose years are counted in the hundreds of millions, you feel once again the sensation of being in a land that is old beyond comprehension. But the evidence is here, written into the rocks from Cap Tourmente to Newfoundland.

One million years ago, a great mantle of ice reached down from the Arctic, moving across the land in sheets two miles thick, crushing and scoring the rock with inching, grinding pressures, and carving out immense valleys throughout Newfoundland, Labrador, and the St. Lawrence region. As the last of the glaciers retreated, they left behind a magnificient legacy of valleys and glacial fiords. Today, the Saguenay River flows through one of the most spectacular fiords on the eastern side of the North American continent. And on the west coast of Newfoundland, a group of U-shaped glacial valleys a few miles inland from the sea forms the heart of Gros Morne National Park. The largest of these valleys, Western Brook Pond, is

△
These wind pruned trees are slowly re-emerging after years of burial beneath coastal sand dunes along Newfoundland's west coast. As the dunes move on they bury living trees and release the old ones. Such graceful shapes are an inspiration to a former member of Canada's National Ballet Company.

△
The walls of Western Brook Pond in Gros Morne National Park rise 2,000 feet above fresh water a few miles inland from the sea, near Newfoundland's west coast. Like the Saguenay fiord, this glacial chasm is a reminder of the immense forces at work during the ice ages.

eight miles long, with sheer rock walls rising almost vertically for 2,000 feet. Hike into Western Brook over trails that wind through sub-arctic bog and old twisted trees, and paddle beneath those great towering walls. You will find it hard to believe you are in Newfoundland.

There is an even more vivid reminder in the St. Lawrence Gulf of the ages of ice and glacier long past. Each summer massive icebergs sweep past the shores of Labrador, carried down from the high Arctic on the Labrador Current. Many of them slip through the Strait of Belle Isle and float majestically into the Gulf. Others grind up on Newfoundland's eastern shore or anchor firmly in deep, sheltered bays where they decay and break up through the summer months. These grounded 'bergs are unwelcome visitors. They play havoc with fishermen's nets, and stories are told of those that split suddenly or roll over, sending up giant waves, a constant hazard for small boats. Few sights in Canada are more impressive than this annual silent procession of porcelain-white mountains drifting quietly and ominously down the Atlantic coast and into the Gulf, primitive relics of the colossal forces that centuries ago shaped and molded the land of the St. Lawrence.

Our brief journey to the St. Lawrence region left us with a patchwork quilt of impressions. The land is far larger than we had imagined and enriched by its close relationship with the sea. It is an ancient region, changed by geological and human history, yet always waiting to be discovered anew. Explore the land of the St. Lawrence. Follow the river's course from Cap Tourmente to the Gaspé Peninsula. Cross the living Gulf and travel the road that soon runs out on the north shore. You will find, as we did, that the land of the St. Lawrence is a land few people know well.

1◁
2▽

3▽

4▽

5▽

6▽
7▷
8▷

9 ▷

Images Of Baffin

The sun brushes soft colour
into the superb Arctic landscape.
Through a macro lens the tundra comes alive
with the wild colours of tiny plant communities.
In the harsh majesty of this immense land,
the true colour and beauty are at your feet.
We find caribou antlers,
easily 100 years old,
painted with lichens
and woven into the fabric of the tundra vegetation.

It is cold in the tent. The calendar says July 29, and for the past two hours soft slithers on the cotton walls have whispered of wet snow. The wind that howled over the tundra most of the night has died away, and inside two fluffy sleeping bags there is nothing but delicious warmth. The soft tundra mosses beneath seem to be embracing us. We are wonderfully alone, a few degrees above the Arctic Circle, more than sixty miles from the nearest community. We have slept for ten hours.

A lemming went through our packs in the night. We heard him out there, heard the excited scufflings as he found the food box, the tiny buzz-saw munchings as he tried some freeze-dried vegetables. Will he swell up like a balloon as they "rehydrate" inside his stomach? Tomorrow Janet will try to tame him, and the tent will be surreptitiously surrounded with little pieces of bread. You can't let a lemming go hungry in the night.

△
Pangnirtung Pass is ringed with sharp mountain peaks and ridges, some of which are table-topped, like Mount Asgaard, with sheer walls and the general shape of an upside-down tumbler. This region of Baffin Island forms the eastern edge of the Canadian Shield.

△
A young Arctic hare dodges away among the boulders of Owl Valley, avoiding the attentions of his first human visitor. By moving slowly, and speaking softly, Janet was able to approach within five feet.

We crawl reluctantly out into two inches of wet snow. A three thousand foot wall of rock has disappeared in the night, lost somewhere in the mist that is rolling silently through Owl Valley. The sense of isolation is complete. A milky sun glimmers and disappears, and a single snowy owl ghosts over the tundra, a white wraith, sudden death for lemmings.

Isolation and bad weather have stolen us a few days of peace in the middle of a busy month of filming. We are marooned here. The chopper can't make it back through the wicked foggy contours of the mountain pass, and it is with a certain joy that we switch on the radio and report our weather to Pangnirtung: "Visibility zero; ceiling zero." Time for breakfast. But the voice of conscience whispers inside; we crank up the Bolex and film a few scenes of the tent in the snow, the soft beauty of Owl Valley after a summer storm, the soggy, freeze-dried breakfast omelette.

We are startled by a sudden voice on the radio. A geological field party is reporting in, their signal so strong they must be near. They are, about three miles away — and we thought we were alone. For some reason their radio won't raise Pangnirtung, so we relay their message, chat a bit, and plan to hike over. But first, a search for the elusive, young snowy owls that we know are being fed somewhere among the old, lichen-encrusted boulders on the tundra.

The adults are too smart for us. They materialize on rocks ahead, wait until we are fifty yards away, and then shift to another rock, and another, leading us away. We catch on, and reverse our steps, and the owls swoop low overhead, complaining. We search for two hours, our waterproof boots soaked by the boggy tundra. The owls make another pass, and something moves among the rocks. We find him, wrinkling his nose at us from under a giant boulder. It is a young Arctic hare, paying about as much attention to us as he would to a grazing caribou. But he must have developed a permanent crick in the neck from living in a meadow full of owls. We talk to him softly and Janet, ever optimistic, flicks a few dried apple flakes his way. One of them bounces off his nose and he trundles away indignantly. We follow to find him munching on some dwarf willow. This time it's one eye on the owls and one eye on Janet. But we move quietly, filming, photographing, and soon we are within five feet of him. We must surely be his first human beings. His fur is a superb blends of greys, his ears tipped with black. If he survives those owls he'll turn pure white by winter. When he moves he is all feet and ears. Casually he starts to groom, lifting one immense, furry foot, and chews delicately around his toes.

The sun begins to brush soft colour into this superb Arctic landscape. Through a macro lens the tundra comes alive with the wild colours of tiny plant communities. In the harsh majesty of this immense land, the true colour and beauty are at your feet. We find caribou antlers, easily 100 years old, painted with lichens and woven into the fabric of the tundra vegetation.

We unexpectedly discover a tent among the rocks and are amazed to see a small child. He belongs to one of the geologists who has brought his family with him. We share a cup of tea and talk. They have been here three weeks but now are anxious to move out, to stand under a hot shower and forget about the ten days of rain and snow and damp sleeping bags. Two weeks later we learn that they left all of their garbage behind, sitting on the tundra in cardboard boxes. It is said that in the Arctic a piece of paper lasts for years, a wooden crate for decades. How can scientists, who should understand these Arctic realities, simply walk away from their own garbage?

Back at our own camp, a rare sight. A peregrine falcon, less than 100 feet away, streaks over the land and pounces on some luckless creature in a dry stream bed. It is too dark for pictures, the light meter says "go home". We also notice something else, now that the mist has gone. We are camped at the edge of a recent landslide. Sometime in the spring the rocks and soil tore away and swept across the slope with such fury that granite boulders have been shattered and pulverized into pink dust. We scramble over the slide, marvelling at the forces that were released, and warily eyeing the slopes above our tent. Half a mile of devastation. It must have been a fantastic sight, but every pebble that moves tonight is going to wake us up.

We light the Coleman Stove, reflecting wistfully on campfires we have known, for a land without trees has no firewood. Camping without a fire is like missing a friend who should have been there. The freeze-dried chicken stew, which we have been avoiding for two summers, goes back into the pack, and we make chili con carne instead. Maybe we can train that lemming to eat chicken stew.

Grey dusk creeps over the land, and Owl Valley becomes a moonscape. A peaceful night, but the morning weather looks uncertain, and at 7 o'clock we radio Pangnirtung. We have been separated from our film crew for three days, and we worry about moving on, shooting film. The helicopter is available; we request a fast pick-up before the mountain pass fills in again. Our transmission ends and we listen, fascinated, as scientific field parties call in, some of them 100 miles away.

They exchange information, request supplies or a move by helicopter to another valley, joke, gossip and sign off. Like a spider reaching all corners of its web, the voice on the radio touches them all, taking the edge off their isolation.

A distant, whistling hum, a roar, and the Hughes 500 settles among the rocks. Our idyll has ended, and it's time to get back to work.

We rose slowly above Owl Valley, above an ancient landscape that has acquired a new status. This is the heart of the world's first truly Arctic national park. Aujuituq (pronounced ow-you-we-took) National Park, 8,300 square miles reaching north and south across the Arctic Circle on Baffin Island's Cumberland Peninsula, and named for the Inuit word that means, "Land of the big ice", or "Place where the snow never melts".

The name is well chosen, for this part of Baffin is a land carved and shattered by three ice ages, a land still emerging from the last ice age. It is a wild blend of jagged rock and living glaciers, whose frozen tongues reach around the mountains on all sides into the valleys and fiords of Cumberland Peninsula. No roads cut the landscape, no casual bulldozer track scars the tundra. Generations of Inuit people have hunted the coastline and made forays inland for caribou, but few other men have passed this way.

▷

A common sight in Owl Valley, caribou antlers almost covered by slow growing tundra vegetation. These antlers may be a hundred years old, but the herds that once roamed here have dwindled after methodical hunting over many seasons.

You can enter this wilderness on foot, at the end of an icy, salt water fiord, only twelve miles from the hamlet of Pangnirtung. Here the mountains rear into the sky more than a mile above you, their progress unhindered by trees or vegetation. Great walls of 600-million-year-old rock, littered with the debris of boulders torn loose by the last ice age, stand above the valley. Hanging glaciers loom among the canyons, feeding the icy streams at your feet. It is not a gentle land, but this trail of ice and boulders and sliding glacial moraines must surely become the greatest hiking trail in the world. If you have the legs, the endurance and the supplies, you can walk from here clean across the Cumberland Peninsula to Davis Strait. You will meet the snowy owls and the Arctic hare in Owl Valley, hear the falcons scream among granite towers, feel your feet crunching among the lichens and sponging into the tundra beside the Owl River. The rumble of falling rock is a sound you will never

quite get used to, and you should remember the warnings not to pitch your tent under an overhang. You will have to wade the streams, and you will gasp with the shock of water that carries memories of a thousand Arctic winters.

Just one more hazard awaits you here, in Pangnirtung Pass — wind. The valley is narrow and wind funnels though with a violence that can hardly be described. One hiker who spent some time in Pangnirtung Pass, a seasoned, athletic type with some knowledge of these conditions, doubled up his tent poles as a precaution. Both snapped the first night. And he remembered trying to drink from a cup while silt whipped horizontally through the air like buckshot: "You keep one hand over the cup, raise your palm slightly and sip quickly". Yet he was filled with the exhilaration of one who has glimpsed a true wilderness, for Pangnirtung Pass is raw, elemental nature, overpowering, magnificently wild. Because there are no trees to soften and soothe the transition from valley floor to mountain, you feel the closeness and the power of the rubble strewn slopes that sweep up on every side. It is a land for wide angle lenses and every superlative you can coax from your memory, and on those days when the winds are calm and the clouds stop smoking among the peaks 5,000 feet above, you will glimpse something else—a white dome, lapping over the mountain tops like frozen surf — the ancient Penny Ice Cap.

The helicopter climbed slowly, rotor blades whistling through thin, cold air. At five thousand feet we were among the peaks and the world began to turn white. Bill Cheffins shouted in my ear: "We're going to try to set her down right on top of the ice cap". Bill was our guide and counsellor, a talented planner from Parks Canada. It was Bill's research and exploration that determined the boundaries of this park.

Suddenly, the world went back in time. We looked down on a land buried beneath a mile-thick mantle of ice rolling away to the horizon in glowing, white contours. We hovered above 2,400 square miles of ice, a remnant of the great Wisconsin Glacier. This is how it was in southern Canada 15,000 years ago. Somewhere beneath the ice cap is a landscape that no man has ever seen.

We touched down briefly. Our cameraman, Bob Ryan, worked quickly, once again capturing a vast land and rolling it up inside his camera at twenty-four frames a second. But the weather was uncertain, the pilot anxious to move on, away from

△
A two hundred foot wall of unstable ice at the edge of a great glacier that reaches down from the Penny Ice Cap. There is an abrupt and dramatic transition here from ice to granite rock.

this eerie, dangerous plateau where storms can materialize in minutes. We fell away into the valleys again, "flying like a mosquito", as one Inuit would say later. And then the strange shape of Mount Asgaard stood before us, like an upside-down tumbler, smooth on every side, flat on top.

There is a legend about Mount Asgaard — not your average thousand-year-old legend, but a little more recent, about three years to be exact. The tale, as told by a park planner, concerns a giant creature who is said to live at the top of Asgaard. You've heard of Chicken Little? Well, up there, on Asgaard, lives that great bird of the north, Ptarmigan Little, and Ptarmigan Little controls all of the weather in the new national park. We can hardly wait to read about him in the official park literature.

Ptarmigan Little was in one of his better moods on this day, and we decided to use the fine weather to film areas that we could never have reached under marginal conditions. We invaded the peace of Owl Valley once more, gave the chopper a drink from a fuel cache, and whirled across the edge of the Penny Ice Cap to the beautiful Coronation Glacier, a vast river of ice trapped between vertical rock walls, spilling its gleaming load into the salt waters of Coronation Fiord. It was low tide, and a strip of silty beach offered a landing site. A single seal, all eyes and whiskers, glided like a beaver in the blue water. We had planned to camp there, but at once we saw that it was too dangerous. The glacier had been busy rearranging the rocks, pushing up walls of sand and dumping tons of ice in the fiord. If we had stayed, there is every chance our camp would have been rearranged. It is an unstable and wildly beautiful place, where the basic elements of an Arctic coast come together — rock, ice, silt and salt water.

Bob Ryan began to rope himself into place in the helicopter door. He was more outside than in, but securely tied down, with safety cords attached to his camera, his light meter, and even his hat. Everything that was loose or could be dislodged by the slipstream was removed from the open doorway, and the pilot ran a final, careful inspection to make sure that nothing could fly back into the delicate tail rotor. Bob stepped out onto the pontoon to check his freedom of movement. This was how he would shoot, looking forward at the rugged Arctic landscape as it raced towards him.

We turned away from the blast of sand as the chopper rose up and away to shoot aerials among the cliffs that cradle the glacier. We had stayed on the ground to

△
Bob Ryan in shooting position. He is firmly roped in place, with enough freedom to move in and out of the doorway. Safety cords are attached to his light meter and his hat to prevent them from accidently blowing into the helicopter's delicate tail rotor. He can shoot in any direction and with more flexibility than a gyroscopic camera mount costing thousands of dollars.

△
Inuit children in Pangnirtung. The sight of a camera sends them into happy laughter and a marvellous variety of poses. They are sitting on an excellent painting that someone has left against the side of a house.

▷
Janet recording village sounds with a parabolic microphone and some assistance from the happy-go-lucky and completely captivating children. These children laugh and chatter continually, and love to walk around with visitors, holding their hands and forming long lines reminiscent of a scene from The Pied Piper.

reduce the pilot's load. Standing alone by our little pile of survival gear, watching them grow tiny among 2,000-foot cliffs, we realized that no one else knew we were there. The unspeakable, unthinkable: "If they crash, will anyone ever find us?" The glacier returned to silence. Then again came that whistling hum. The helicopter swept low across the boulder-strewn surface, banked sharply among ice floes in the blue salt water and screamed gently back to earth. There was laughter and excitement at the "impossible" manoeuvres Bob had coaxed from the pilot. We detected some nervousness in that laughter.

Given the budget to hire these great cash registers in the sky, film making in such remote areas is twice as effective. To capture an enormous landscape on film in such a way that television viewers can grasp the size and scale of that land requires movement: not just scenery flashing by the camera, but the imaginative staging of moving foregrounds against great vistas beyond; the sudden surprise of a glacier that seems to burst out from behind pinnacles of rock; the scene that towers away from two tiny figures lost among fifty-ton boulders; the ice cap unravelling before you at 90 mph; the camera that skims and banks through narrow canyons above a wild river. No camera platform can match the helicopter's ability to do these things. To hike into all of these areas on foot would take months, and many of the places we filmed on Baffin Island were virtually inaccesible except by helicopter.

Something white is gleaming among dark grey rocks. We are still a hundred feet above the ground, descending toward the bleak stone surface of Kekerton Island that seems locked into place by the crushing ice pack of Cumberland Sound. There it is again. I feel a shiver of disbelief, but will say nothing until we are down, and I can confirm my suspicions. We peer out with uncertainty, like astronauts who have landed in some dreadful place. There is no wind, no sound, no movement—nothing but rock. We wait inside as the pilot winds down his spinning machinery, until there is silence.

I drift away casually through the boulders, and stop. I was right. In a shallow pool of water among the rocks a human skull grins a quiet greeting. Gentle sadness dissolves away the shiver of apprehension, and there is a moment of silent communication. But who was he? How long has he been here? Where are the rest of his bones? We find a rib bone, a tibia, and finally a broken coffin and a row of faded,

△
The skull of a nineteenth century whaler on the lonely and bleak island of Kekerton. His grave was probably broken open by a passing polar bear. After a few experiences like this we became accustomed to the sight of human bones in old settlements.

weathered markers. These were the whalers of Kekerton Island, the men who died on this lonely Arctic rock, far from the warmth of home and family.

We speculate. Perhaps a polar bear tore the grave open, scattering these white bones over the land. The lettering on the fragile wooden crosses is illegible, but we know that Scottish whalers came here in the 1850's, and built a permanent whaling station. Inuit families followed, and they too are buried here.

How do you bury someone in a land of cold, unyielding granite? We find the answer on the slopes behind the ruins of their settlement. Two small wooden boxes, side by side and held down by boulders, conceal the bodies of two Inuit children. A few feet away is a large barrel, once used for whale oil, but now the last resting place of an adult. It has been pushed against a slab of rock and partially buried under large stones. Another skull lies on the tundra, close to an open box that contains a skeleton but no head. Gently Janet picks up the skull and restores it to its owner. We feel no sense of dread, but an overwhelming compassion for those who died in this forbidding place. There is a sadness too. We would like to have known them, to hear their laughter, to see them as families. We wonder why their children died. There are too many little boxes.

By the time this tiny settlement came to the barren slopes of Kekerton Island, years of hardship and disaster had traced the erratic fortunes of an uncertain and dangerous pursuit of the great bowhead whale. The final tragedy was the impact on these superb and intelligent creatures of the sea. The bowhead was hunted almost to extinction in these waters, and then the industry turned its attention to the beautiful white whale, the beluga. These gentle mammals were driven into shallow bays at high water and slaughtered as the tides ebbed away with their lives. Their fat was rendered into oil, their flesh given to dogs, their skins sent to England to be turned into boot laces. When you see the white whales today, porpoising gracefully in the milky, blue waters of Cumberland Sound, it is difficult to think of them as so many boot laces. We feel compassion for the men whose lives were tied to such harsh Arctic disciplines, but we cannot in any way find reason for their mission.

We left Kekerton Island, spinning across the sea, whistling over the ice at 100 miles an hour, about ten feet "off the deck". The pilot assured us that his machine rode comfortably on a cushion of air at this low altitude. We smiled nervously and looked for tall ice floes. The wandering walls of Kingnait Fiord closed in on both sides and guided us back to our campsite in a sheltered bay. A team of archaeologists was working there, gently excavating the old houses of Thule Eskimos who had hunted there hundreds of years ago. Stone slabs and pieces of whalebone surrounded by unusually green grass marked the location of each "house", but beyond this there was little left. Again, on rising ground behind the camp, were some of the people who had lived there. More than eighty rock tombs cradled the bones of the first people in this land. We were becoming accustomed to the dull, white glow of skulls among the rocks.

These Thule families had also been whale hunters, but their business had been survival at the edge of an Arctic sea. When European whalers began to invade Thule hunting areas, the Inuit were forced into a more nomadic life and survival became an endless hunt, tempered by a growing scarcity of sea mammals. Their skill and ingenuity overcame dreadful hardship.

The Inuit people of Pangnirtung are direct descendants of those tough and adaptable members of the Thule culture. But few live out in hunt camps today, for settlements such as Pangnirtung are a strong attraction and a comfortable haven during the long, dark days of winter. This remarkably lively little community is just twenty miles south of the Arctic Circle and sheltered by the thrusting walls of Pangnirtung Fiord. Ice floes drift in and out of the fiord, carried by tides and frequent gale-force winds. Just twelve miles away the hills become mountains. The combined elements of blue salt water and pale, sparkling ice beneath the misty slopes of Pangnirtung Pass offer visitors a spectacular view as they step out of small aircraft on Pangnirtung's gravel strip. This airstrip brings people, mail and freight two or three times a week. Once a year supply ships arrive among the drifting ice floes to give the community its annual transfusion of oil, gasoline, clothing, canned goods, motorbikes, snowmobiles, building materials, frozen meat, soft drinks—an endless list of community and personal needs. Twelve months of supplies arrive in one delivery. Small wonder the Hudson's Bay store is almost empty before "sealift" arrives. This expensive isolation drives prices up—bed and board at the little hotel was a budget-straining fifty dollars a day for each member of our crew.

The short Arctic summer comes to Pangnirtung in a celebration of long days and brilliant sunsets. In these few weeks it seems as though no one goes to bed early, and the sound of children's laughter echoes through all hours of the night. Perhaps

△
A rare sight in Pangnirtung, where the eighteen-foot, square stern canoe and forty HP motor has completely replaced the kayak. This kayak is kept as an artifact in the Co-op store, but some of the older men look at its graceful lines, and remember.

▷
Markoosie Pitseolak, or "Sea Pigeon", paddling the only kayak in Pangnirtung. He is in his eighties and thoroughly enjoying himself, as he demonstrates skills learned during a lifetime in hunt camps at the edge of the sea.

they are all too aware that even at the height of summer winter is never far away. Perhaps they remember those long shivering months when the sun hides behind the mountains, and the Arctic wind comes screaming up the fiord out of the darkness to tear at the steel cables anchoring the little houses of Pangnirtung.

The winters may be cruel, but the young Inuit today knows little of the hardships of a year-round life in hunting camps. The old people, however, remember. Markoosie Pitseolak was in this eighties when we met him. Through an interpreter we heard of his life around the forbidding shorelines of Cumberland Sound, during all seasons and far from the comforts of this settlement. With great good humour and delight he took the only kayak in Pangnirtung out into the icy waves of the fiord and showed us that the old skills are never forgotten. We were told that Pitseolak means "sea pigeon", and Markoosie was indeed flying, at one with the water that had given him life for so many years.

Perhaps the cheerful good humour of the Inuit people has helped them to survive centuries of hardship. Certainly, behind that humour is a remarkable level of ingenuity, inventiveness and high intelligence. Today, Pangnirtung's Inuit council runs the community and is involved in all major decisions affecting planning and future development. Winds of change — notably the new national park on their doorstep—have been a source of some concern for members of the council, who are far more wary about the sociological impact of new development than their counterparts in southern communities.

Today Pangnirtung sits on the threshold of 8,300 square miles of superb and uncompromising Arctic wilderness park. For some visitors, a few days in Pangnirtung itself can be equally as interesting as a hike into the park, providing them with a glimpse of life in an Arctic community.

Aujuituq National Park is not a place for inexperienced travellers, but if you are physically fit and accustomed to the hardships of wilderness back-packing, it is a place you will never forget. There will be no helicopter to whisk you about, and you will be only as good as your hiking boots and your muscles. It is precisely this kind of challenge that makes the park so worthwhile, and so impressive.

▷
A magnificent whale bone carving at Pangnirtung. The carving is made from the entire skull of a whale and stands about three feet high. With a symbolism perhaps known only to himself, the artist has enclosed the figures within the open mouth of a walrus. Whales were heavily hunted in Cumberland Sound for many years.

1◁

2▷

3▽

4▽

5◁

6▽
7▷

8▽

9 ▷

To go into the quiet of woods or mountains produces a feeling of perfect rest and liberation — a true re-creation. In such surroundings many long dormant faculties are brought into play. Almost every sensation travels along old grooves worn in the minds of long past generations. A person finds pleasure in the absolute stillness, in primitive and wild sounds such as the wind in the trees, the falling of water, the wide expanse of landscape or sky, and he renews again his ancient relationship with wild animals, a relationship as old as man himself.

James B Harkin
Dominion Parks Commissioner,
Annual Report, 1917